I0554937

English & Spanish

MANNERS    ETIQUETTE
MODALES    ETIQUETA

SELF ESTEEM
AUTOESTIMA

4 "U"

&

"M&E"

BY: BARBARA GIBSON LA'GRANT

ALFRBA

Manners Etiquette Self-Esteem for "U" and "M&E"

Modales Etiqueta Autoestima English & Spanish

Copyright © 2023 by Barbara Gibson La'Grant

ALL RIGHTS RESERVED.

No part of this publication may be copied or reproduced, for commercial gain or profit, except for brief quotations in printed reviews. The material may not be stored in a retrieval system, or any form or by any means, transmitted electronically, mechanical, photocopying, recording, or otherwise, without the publisher's or author's prior written consent.

ISBN: 978-1-958117-11-8

Published By: JATNE Publishing, LLC

Printed in the United States of America

# Table of Contents

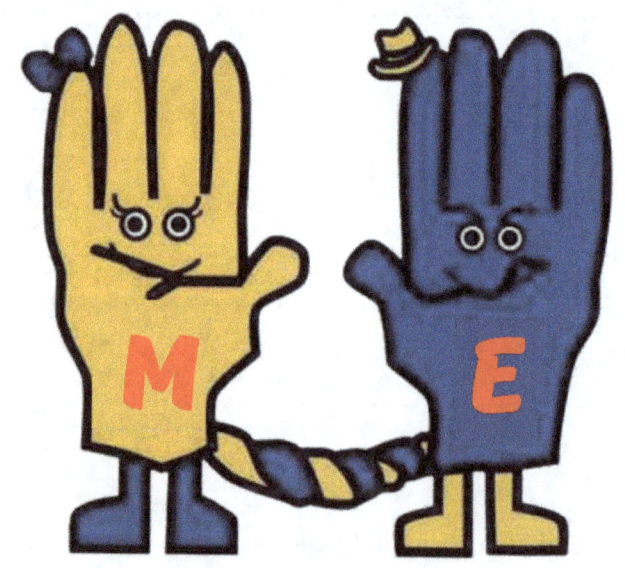

MS. MANNERS & MR. ETIQUETTE

# Dedication

Thank you to the many people I've connected with on this journey. They have helped me evolve into the person I am today.

To my husband for always supporting me one hundred percent with the ''ALFRBA'' crew at every Bronx Day Parade, Jo's Printing for giving us the look of the 'BX' Bronx Love.

To my wonderful siblings, sister Fredtrine Jefferies, and brother Alfred Jefferies. The first two letters of our names created the family business name "ALFRBA." (Pronounced: al fr ba)

To our mother of three, a self-described "southerner". Kathreen Jefferies didn't take any mess. She instilled within me the SOCIAL-LIFE-SELF-SKILLS that I share with "U."

I also want to acknowledge my son, Theodore "Teddy" Gibson, and my nephew, Miles Brinson, who have gone on to Heaven. Their lives were short and sweet. "U" are greatly missed by your Family

**MS. MANNERS & MR. ETIQUETTE**

# Introduction

Some may say "yes ma'am" and "no sir" are outdated, but the author believes that **Good Manners** are relevant and needed today.

This book is especially meaningful in an age where dining out is more common and less time is spent at home at the dinner table. "Manners & Etiquette ("M&E") with Self-Esteem" shares three strategies (Manners, Etiquette, and Self-Esteem) for raising our children into successful and positive people. This book will help them grow through all ages and stages.

The author's background sharing, teaching, and empowering her students makes her uniquely qualified to guide parents towards engaging their children's senses to explore the "1,2,3," of Manners, Etiquette, and Self-Esteem through interaction at home.

This book aims to help students build friendships, communicate, and thrive at school, which can power the sense of belonging with others. You want children who are patient, kind, humble, thankful, and respectful, all of which are traits that will help them develop a good work ethic.

Strong character and a healthy self-image help children grow to the best of their ability. "U" can't force a child to be grateful for everything, but "U" can raise a successful, responsible child who grows into an adult that makes their parents proud.

Thank "U" for taking the time to read Barbara Gibson La'Grant's first bilingual book. This will be a good read for parents, teachers, and students.

The mission of this book is to call attention to the need to build Life and Self-Esteem Skills. This book will share insight, answer questions, and give simple instructions to make it easy for Life application.

Careful mindfulness in planning will pay off in learning the "M&E", Social, Life, and Self-Skills. As the world changes, the process is still the same from A to Z, teaching skills like "1,2,3," and believing that every child needs it more today than yesterday.

The author's organization "ALFRBA" works to address and improve Social Skills and believes "M&E" & Self-Esteem" is a must for "U" and "M&E".

Each topic within this book is worthy of deep reflection for a child but is only a starting point. With guidance, our children will learn to stand strong against obstacles as they learn important principles and how to handle themselves.

Ms. Barbara hopes that prioritizing the "1,2,3," of Manners & Etiquette with Self Esteem will have the same effect on your Life that it has had on her.

For many years she has counseled and practiced her craft, creating and presenting various workshops on "M&E" with Self-Esteem. She has longed to put a book like this in the hands of others, which gives children an opportunity to learn two languages, English and Spanish.

These pages have deep wisdom, as Ms. Barbara has found a beautiful way to open up to children. What could be better than having gentle fun with your child while building the foundation for social and emotional balance and success as they grow?

Ms. Barbara believes the best way to support children is to arm their parents with the knowledge and skills on child development for their success during childhood and beyond.

Ms. Barbara has taught about Manners, Etiquette, and Self-Esteem for over thirty years. She believes that Good Manners are a must if a person wants to be successful. In her efforts, she has designed two plush characters in the shape of the alphabets" M" and "E", her trademark. She has also created napkins to go with the plush characters with Spanish and English words on each, helping children learn in a fun way.

This delightful book is shareable as a read-aloud with young children and a way to learn two languages at the same time. Thus, it is two books in one, with separate "English and Spanish" sections. Also, you will see emphasis used throughout of "U" and "M&E."

It's Manners & Etiquette Time..........

"Ms. Manners Meets Mr. Etiquette"

M is for Manners    E is for Etiquette

For You And

"Manners & Etiquette"

Are Forever

ESTAS SON ALGUNAS EXPRESIONES
BILINGÜES UTILIZADAS PARA MOSTRAR
BUENOS MODALES

Yes

Sí

Please

Por Favor

You're Welcome

DeNada

Excuse Me

Perdónenme

Thank You

Gracias

May I

¿Puedo...

I'm Sorry

Lo Siento

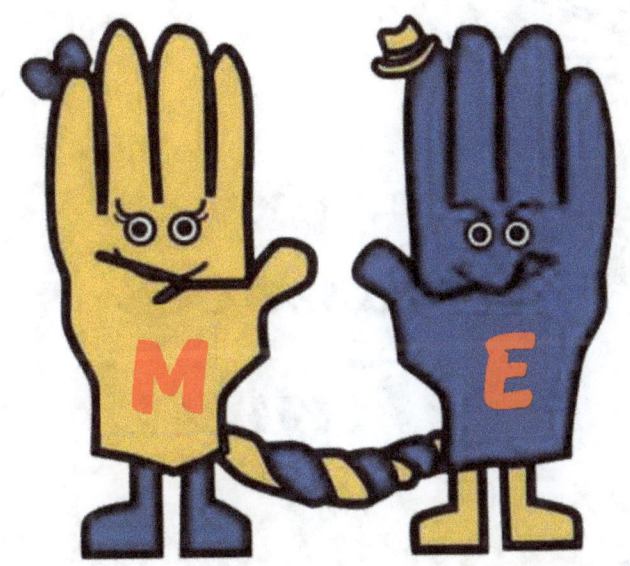

**MS. MANNERS & MR. ETIQUETTE**

It's Manners Time

## Manners & Etiquette with Self-Esteem Pledge

I pledge to use my *Manners* every day.

To say, thank you, you're welcome, and excuse me.

I pledge to say, "How are you?" and "How was your day?"

To say, "good morning", "good afternoon", and "good night",

to my loved ones. I pledge to be polite.

To say, "I'm sorry",

and to remember to care and be kind to my friends.

I pledge to be on my best behavior,

and to be respectful to myself and others.

I pledge to listen and follow directions and to be honest.

I pledge to use my *Etiquette* every day and to

greet others with a Smile.

I pledge to wash my hands before and after a meal,

and to use my napkin.

Also, place my hand on my lap and my elbow off the table.

I pledge to develop my *Self-Esteem* every day.

I will learn how to engage with others,

and become the best person I can be.

## The Importance of Manners

Manners and Etiquette ("M&E") are not the same. "M&E" are different and shouldn't be confused with each other.

- Manners are the outward behaviors that reflect a person's **attitude in a positive human interaction**.
- Etiquette is a standard of conduct with societal rules related to **behavioral interaction** with others.

Manners are life skills that show how a person behaves toward others. Manners are expected and respected by many people. When people show good Manners, they let those around them see that they respect other people's feelings. With good Manners, we are likely to encourage good behavior from other people.

Come on, crew, we have a job to do. Good Manners & Etiquette are Forever.

It would be wise for parents to correct the way their children answer them, and others. Start teaching early.

## Words to Remember

**Excuse ME -** Can be used when there is a need to get someone's attention, to get past someone, to ask someone to repeat what they have just said, or when someone passes another and accidentally bumps into them.

**May I –** Can be used when asking for permission to do something or go somewhere.

**Can I** – Is suitable when asking if "U" can help someone with something. Parents like the use of, "Can I" when the child wants to do something.

**Be Polite** – To have or show behavior that is respectful and considerate of other people. By being polite, children have the opportunity to display their respect for others.

**Be Kind** – Kindness is based on how friendly, generous, and considerate a person is to others.

**Be Neat** – Clean up behind yourself at home and when visiting others. Help to keep public areas clean. Return items to the place you found them.

**Share** – Sharing is the act of taking some of what "U" have (toys, food, games) and giving some of it to another. Sharing with a friend shows them that "U" are not selfish. Show others "U" care about them and their needs/wants.

**Be Thankful –** Expressing gratitude for what "U" have. Being grateful for what "U" own and showing others "U" are thankful.

**Be Happy –** Showing pleasure or contentment with what "U" have. No one has complete control over being happy, but "U" can choose to work daily at being happier.

# MANNERS ARE FOREVER

- Mannerable
- A Good Listener
- Respectful
- Kind
- Polite
- Neat
- On Time

- Please
- Excuse Me
- May I
- I am sorry
- Thank you

# Manners When a Door is Closed

Do the following before entering a room with a closed door.

- Respect others' privacy.
- Knock first.
- Before opening the door make sure you hear someone welcome "U" into the room.
- You may need to wait for the person to open the door.

## When Exiting a Room

- Never slam a door.
- Learn to hold the door and gently close it.
- It is nice to hold the door open for others when entering and leaving a room.

## Manners Are Forever

Manners, like your heart, are with "U" each day. Remember how important it is to think about others and **say I'm sorry right away** if "U" do something wrong to someone, even if it's an accident.

## Manners at Home

Being part of a family can be challenging work, but it's important to always speak to people in a respectful tone of voice. Whether it's your mother, father, sister, or brother, always remember the golden rule of manners, which states, "Do unto others as "U" would have them do unto "U."

Sometimes "U" will have to give a little to get a little. The critical thing is always to be as polite and as understanding as possible.

## Patience is a Virtue

This behavior shows high moral standards. Patience is the ability to wait for something without getting angry or upset; It is an excellent quality in a person. Patience, kindness, and self-control help people become better versions of themselves.

## Doing Chores

You might be in charge of chores around the house, like cleaning your room, washing the dishes, etc. Staying on top of your chores is crucial. If "U" do not complete your chores on time, "U" create more work for yourself. "U" can end up doing twice as much work if it's not done right the first time.

## Volunteer Work

Make each day count and spread the love. Use your skills to help others. Give back a percentage of your time by helping out in your community, expecting nothing in return.

## Smile

If I invite "U" to look in a mirror to see your smile, would "U" smile at yourself?

Try smiling at a passerby. When "U" smile, the person can see the way "U" feel. "U" have no idea how much that one smile can change someone's perspective. "U" can change someone's worst day into a better one with just one heartfelt smile.

Remember that one smile might make that person's day better. It might even cause that individual to smile back at "U" or someone else, causing a trickle effect of happiness.

"U" can complement, congratulate, or praise someone for something they did with a smile. Smiles and compliments go very well together. It could make someone feel good about themselves and appreciated by "U."

## Learn to Touch

There are numerous ways to touch one another, such as hugging or holding hands. "U" can also touch someone with a Thumbs Up, words of encouragement, or a Smile. These are ways to touch each other gently, or today we often use a light fist bump.

## Everyone Can Learn

Be open to learning more. Ask questions and listen to their response. When people answer your questions, be patient and do not talk over them. Wait for them to finish and then reply.

## Giving up a Seat

If "U" are sitting down and "U" notice that a pregnant woman, an elderly person, or a disabled person needs a seat, allow them to take your seat. This small action shows a lot of respect and reverence.

Make sure to take time with each subject, (*Manners, Etiquette,* and *Self-Esteem*), so that "U" are getting all the information "U" need. There is no limit to how much "U" can learn with practice.

It's Manners & Etiquette Time..........

"Ms. Manners Meets Mr. Etiquette"

M is for Manners     E is for Etiquette

For You And

"Manners & Etiquette"

Are Forever

# Manners & Etiquette

Manners and Etiquette go together like two hands.

When you say thank "U", that's Manners.

When "U" use your fork and knife instead of your hands,

that's Etiquette.

Now "U" see how Manners & Etiquette can go together.

Always remember the people who helped

"U" along the way. Don't forget to lift

someone else up to pay it forward.

# Manners Reminders

- Being rude is never acceptable. If a rude person is around, try to move from their presence.
- Be on time. If you say "U" will be someplace people expect "U" there. Do what "U" said you would do.
- Don't Tease others. Remember to play and have fun but don't make fun of others. Don't be playful or laugh at or joke about them to upset them.
- Respect yourself and others. Remember, the words "U" use can come back and hurt "U" too.
- No foul language. Offensive words like swearing, cursing, or using rude comments are unacceptable.

## Bullying, Teasing, and more...

Bullying is NO joke.

Did "U" hear ME?

Bullying is NO joke.

I am a Boy that knows a Girl,

and bullying is NO joke for HER or ME.

We both know how it feels, so take it from us.

It's real.

Respect your friend and others too.

Bullying hurts, and it can hurt "U".

Bullying can happen at school, outside,

and even at home.

Cyberbullying or online Bullying is bad too.

Did "U" hear "M&E"? Bullying is NO joke.

Remember to respect your friends and others.

"U" don't want disrespect to come back

and harm "U" too.

Did "U" hear "M&E"?

Bullying is NO joke.

Manners are Forever. It is good Manners',
to follow proper Etiquette. It's a life principle; you are ready.

"*It's To The Point*" *Use Them*. **RESPECT.**

**MS. MANNERS & MR. ETIQUETTE**

It's Etiquette Time

# The Importance of Etiquette

Etiquette is the customary code of polite behavior in society or among members of a particular profession or group. In social settings, respect yourself and everyone else at a dinner table.

Today, the rules of etiquette are changing, often overlapping in our society. Etiquette presents our conduct, value, and respect for others at home or in a public setting. It shows our **Life Skills**.

## Table Setting

When "U" sit at a table for dinner, "U" will know by the setting what type of food is being served. "U" will also know what utensils to use, and the correct way. You may see one, two, or three forks to the left of your plate. The silverware is placed from the (outside) with the silverware (inward) to the plate.

When looking at the placement of the utensils, which fork is on the outside? "U" will use them from the outside in. If the smaller salad fork is on the outside, "U" will be served salad before the main course. The main course is first if the salad fork is on the inside.

Whichever it is, the basics are the same no matter how many of each utensil or how fancy the tableware is; start from the (outside) and work (inward) with each course.

Here is a friendly reminder on tableside Manners & Etiquette. The following are some things to remember.

**Be On Time When Invited To Dinner**

- It is essential to always be on time; being late is not polite. Start a little early to show up when expected.
- Etiquette is about more than which silverware to use.
- Etiquette's true purpose is always to show respect and kindness.
- For children, Etiquette starts at the doors and goes to the tables as they sit with others.

# Family Style Service

When it is time to sit for the meal, pull your chair out carefully (go in on the left and out on the right). Be sure to pull your chair close to the table if others need to pass by.

A table's setting is all about the order. A dinner plate is in front of each person. The food should be passed in a clockwise direction, to your right. Pass all the dishes in the same direction. To start, pass the food to your right. Hold the container for the person on their right and pass it. If you are first, serve yourself a little bit, then start the passing but ask the person on your left if they would like something. If they say yes, "U" serve them first – not yourself.

Avoid reaching across someone to get a dish. If "U" want something from the table, be polite, and ask someone to Please Pass. Always remember to say Thank "U" to the person when they hand "U" the dish.

## Simple or Fancy Dinner

When "U" sit, know to look at the setting. In a formal setting, there will be charger plates or service plates, which are large plates set underneath the dinner plate. Service plates keep the tablecloth clean. They are kept throughout the meal.

## Viewing the Table

On the table, "U" may see a colorful napkin in one of the glasses and maybe some candles. This is the making of a beautiful table setting. You'll also see the silverware on the table. Remember to use silverware from the (outside) inward. Silverware should not touch the table. After eating the plate is typically removed by the server.

# CONVERSATIONAL NAPKIN

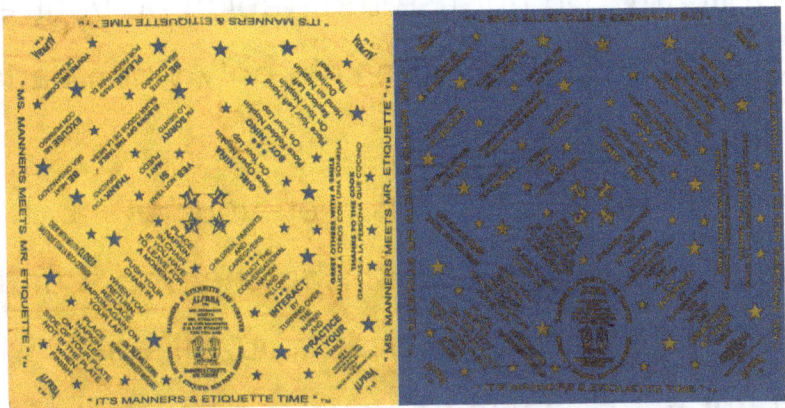

## The Napkin

As soon as you are seated, using your Left Hand, it is proper Etiquette to put your Napkin on your lap as soon as you receive it. It remains there throughout the meal, used only to keep your mouth clean.

- Female use of the Napkin is to be **Opened** completely.
- Male use of the Napkins is to be **Folded** in half.
- The Napkin remains in the lap – never place it on the table until the meal is finished.

- Use the Napkin to remove extra food or sauce from your mouth lightly. Do not use the Napkin on your entire face.
- Tuck the Napkin under the chin only when eating seafood or spaghetti.
- Remember to put the Napkin on your chair when temporarily leaving the table, then push the chair back under the table.
- When "U" return to your seat, you will again with your Left Hand put your Napkin on your Lap.
- Remember, to always sit "UP" straight, and never slump.
- When ending the meal, place the napkin on the left side of your plate, then get up and push your chair under the table. This will let the staff know "U" are finished with the meal.

## Glasses

Whether a fancy or simple table setting, there will always be three glasses to each place setting. There will be one for water, and two wine glasses. They may not get used, but this is the standard setting for glasses on the table. The flute glasses are used for sparkling wine.

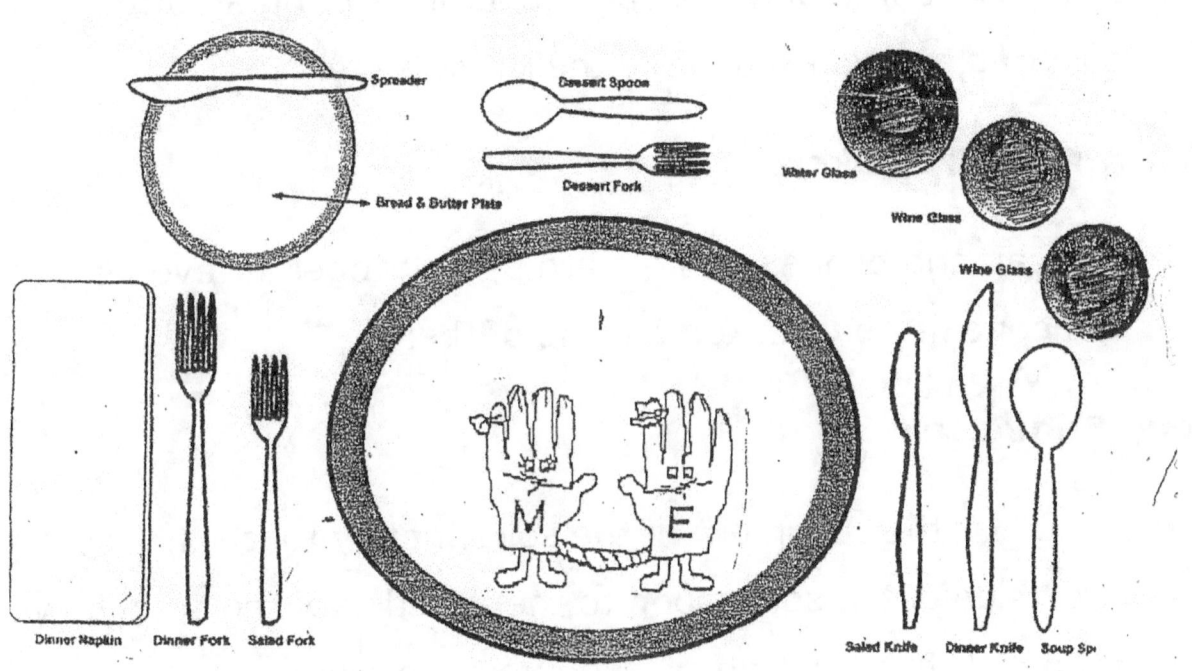

## Bread and Butter

- Share the butter dish.
- Use a butter knife to put the butter on your plate.
- The breadbasket usually holds one portion per person.
- Make sure only to touch your portion.
- Break bread (don't cut) off one bite-size piece at a time.
- It is essential to only take a second piece of bread after ensuring everyone can take their first piece.

## Salt & Pepper Shakers

- The salt and pepper shakers are passed together even if someone has only asked for one of them.

## Soup Etiquette

- As "U" lift the spoon out of the soup, gently touch the underside of the soupspoon to the far edge of the soup bowl.
- Keeps "U" from spilling soup on your clothing.

- When finished eating, always rest the spoon on the plate below the bowl, not in the bowl.
- Parents or children should practice the soup routine together. Once learned, you'll feel comfortable with this eating method.

## Asian Soup

- In certain Asian communities, smacking lips when eating food is normal. It is also normal to slurp noodles or soups. In the USA, making sounds when eating is considered bad **Manners**. To these Asian people, it is usually polite to slurp or make noises while eating. It is considered best when enjoyed loudly. It is a sign of appreciation to the chef for the Asian people. Adjust your eating style to the area, restaurant, or home "U" are in.

## No Double Dipping

- Never dip food in a sauce, take a bite, and then put it back in a sauce.
- Only dip uneaten pieces of your food into a sauce.

## Praying Before Eating

At some dinner gatherings, a prayer of gratitude may be shared. The host may choose to recite a prayer, as well, before eating. "U" may even be asked to do the prayer. If "U" are uncomfortable doing so, "U" can politely say no.

## At The Table

Greet others with a smile or say hello. It is also okay to have a bit of small talk.

- Be respectful and kind. Always respect yourself and others.
- Sit back to enjoy a good meal and conversation.
- Keep your elbows off the table.

- Having your elbows on the table may be acceptable in a familiar setting. Look to see what the host is doing.

## Eating Your Food
- Slightly lean over your plate as "U" eat so that any spilled food will land on your plate instead of your lap.
- It is a good practice to chew with your mouth closed. Chewing with your mouth open is not polite.
- Never speak while chewing.
- Don't play or sing at the dinner table.

## Cutting Your Food

If "U" will likely have to cut it into bite-sized pieces. Holding the knife and fork right will give "U" the most control over the food on your plate.

## The Knife Reminder

- The cutting edge should face in toward the plate during the meal.

- Transfer the fork to your right hand with the tines up.
- Hold the knife in your left hand and push the food onto your fork. Your knife is also needed to help get bites onto the fork and hold your knife. It is okay to use a fork and no knife.

## Etiquette in Different Cultural Settings

"U" may find yourself in a situation where the food being served is entirely new to "U." Many foods, spices, and herbs are acquired tastes, so don't be surprised if "U" don't like everything. Chinese food might be your favorite, but how do "U" feel about Sushi? Soul Food, Spanish, Jamaican, African, Indian, Italian, or Middle Eastern are options too. There are many types of food in our world! Here are some things to remember when trying new foods.

- Refrain from criticizing the food.
- It's polite to try at least a little of everything.
- Be careful not to react poorly if someone says, "Oh, that's an eel," and an eel is not something "U" have eaten before.

You don't want to say, "Ugh!" Instead, say, "No Thank "U".
Be polite, and say, "I'll try another dish.

## Eating Spaghetti

- Twirl the noodles around with your fork. You can also cut the spaghetti into bite-sized portions.

## Eating Lobster & Claws

- Put a bib on or hang a napkin from your neck.
- "U" may use the fish fork to get the meat out of the claws.

## Fat Meat Etiquette

Sometimes the food may have fat or gristle, which may be hard to chew. Bring your napkin to your mouth and put the meat into the napkin. Then place the item on the edge of your plate.

## The Two Knife Styles

Continental and European

- Continental

- Resting and Finished Style

Have "U" wondered how to place your cutlery on the table or your plate? Should you cross them or place them on the side of your plate, or should they be kept with the cutting-edge face-up?

How your cutlery is put on the plate determines if "U" are asking for more food or saying that "U" are done with your meal.

## Continental Style

The Continental Style dining position has the fork tips and knife edge facing downward.

Resting vs. Finish

- I am finished.

- Keeping the cutlery parallel to each other.

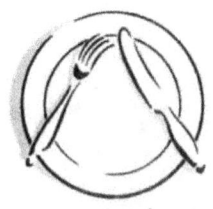

Continental
Resting Position

Continental
Finished Position

## American Style

In American Style dining, position the fork downward. This is the order in which one of these styles appears on your plate. The American style (though the tines must be down), or "U" may place the fork tines down so that they form an X.

- American Style
- Resting vs. Finished

American Resting Position     American Finished Position

The American method starts just like the continental method. Still, the difference is that when "U" have finished cutting the meat, "U" put your knife down at the top of the plate with the blade facing toward the center.

If "U" dine in the American style, situate the knife just as "U" are finished with your meal. The fork tines may be up or down alongside the left edge of the knife.

**Finishing The Food**

- American Resting position

**American**
**Resting Position**

- Continental Resting position

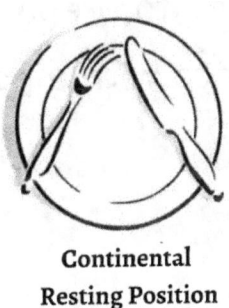

**Continental**
**Resting Position**

It's debated whether or not to finish all the food on your plate. Eat what "U" can, and never overeat. If "U" are hungry enough, feel free to clean your plate! "Bon Appetite".

## The Dinner Has Ended

- Dessert is served when dinner is complete.

- The dinner plates are removed.
- Dessert may be served in a different, more relaxed setting.

**Remember the following:**

- Practice makes perfect.
- Invite a friend and start practicing at home to prepare for your next fancy or simple dining experience with a personal touch.
- Arrive and depart on time.
- Be neat and clean up after yourself.
- The personal touch after the meal.
- Applaud the server or cook for the meal.
- The applause is at the end of the meal, where "U" may clap your hands as an expression of approval, like ending a performance. Try to pay attention and be in sync with those around "U."
- When leaving the meal, say, thank "U" to the cook or host.

- Thank "U" notes are always welcome.
- Remember, Manners, Politeness, and The Golden Rule apply.

Manners & Etiquette go Together like "Two Hands."

It's Manners & Etiquette Time..........

"Ms. Manners Meets Mr. Etiquette"

M is for Manners    E is for Etiquette

For You And

"Manners & Etiquette"

Are Forever

Above is the original picture for Manners and Etiquette before Self-Esteem was added to the program flow.

## Conversational Two-Plush Characters

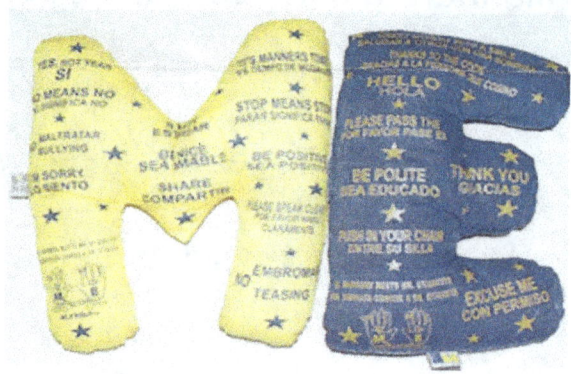

The golden rule is often taught by parents and teachers, and says, "Do unto others as "U" would have others do unto "U" How is this possible? Always remember:

- Be kind.
- Be generous.
- Be considerate.

Always take your Manners & Etiquette along.

They overlap each other in so many ways.

The information shared will guide "U."

**It's To The Point**

**"U"** Are Ready.

Manners & Etiquette Go Together.

**"Bon Appetite"**

It's
Self-Esteem
Time

# SELF-ESTEEM

It is time to change your behavior.

"U" have a choice.

Have confidence in yourself!

Deal with your mistakes.

Learn from your mistakes.

**Dream Big**.

Set Goals.

Pursue your desires.

Give it all you've got!

## The Importance of Self-Esteem

### "Believe in Yourself"

"U" have the ability to believe in yourself. "U" can overcome self–doubt and gain confidence to act and get things done. Realize that all things may not go right, but "U" can work through it towards something different. Evaluate your own worth.

- Self-Esteem provides us with belief in our abilities and motivation to carry them out to reach a positive outlook.
- Self-Esteem is the value or worth "U" feel about yourself.
- Self-Esteem is a basic human need for motivation and to build success.
- Self-Esteem helps us gain and maintain a high regard for ourselves.
- Self-Esteem serves as a protective function throughout life.

Multiple types of Self-Esteem exist, but they are not all the same.

## Three Types of Self-Esteem

1. **High Self-Esteem** – People with this type of self-esteem tend to accept themselves and their abilities confidently. They are willing to give and receive a compliment, believing in one's own worth or ability.

2. **Inflated Self-Esteem** – this person thinks of themselves as better than others and is always ready to underestimate

others. Their behavior can be negative, especially when they do whatever it takes to get ahead of someone else. They don't typically form meaningful and healthy relationships.

3. **Low Self-Esteem** – being too critical and not liking yourself. Thinking others are better than "U" are. Negatively joking about yourself. Ignoring your achievements.

Each person must learn to love themself. Know that "U" are somebody, and "U" can do whatever you set your mind to. In this process, it is important to know:

- Why do you exist?
- Know where "U" are going.
- Be willing to learn from your mistakes.
- Stop running from the past.
- Have the willingness to make new friends.
- Keep the faith and trust yourself in the process.
- Learn to focus on doing and being better.
- Keep going, stay strong, and have a goal.

- Complete what "U" set out to do.

Speak life over yourself and say:

- I am confident.
- I am worthy.
- I am valuable.
- I am strong.
- I am loved.

In the process of developing Self-Esteem, "U" will learn the following:

- Self-worth is the internal sense of belonging, being good enough, and worthy of love from others.
- Self-regarding is the act of respecting yourself. "U" cannot expect from others what "U" are not willing to give to yourself.
- Self-respect is having pride and honoring yourself.

- Self-integrity is having strong morals or values and following those principles in what "U" say and your **actions**.

People, especially children, must know the meaning of Self-Esteem. Share ways with them to improve where they are lacking. Teach children:

- What is right from wrong, to set **good morals**.
- How to pick positive friends that lift them up and not tear them down.
- They can say no and not follow the behavior of others.
- To celebrate with others when good things happen to them.

## Positive Role Model

Everyone needs someone they can look up to. A positive role model inspires others to live meaningful lives. They are a positive example of how to:

- Live with integrity.
- Stay optimistic.

- Be hopeful.
- Have determination.
- Have compassion.
- Hold yourself and your work to a high standard.
- Set a good example.

"U" too can be a role model!

Without standards in our lives, everything would be out of control. Setting a standard is designed to be used as a rule or guideline. Standards have to be developed, such as Manners & Etiquette & Self-Esteem. Try our standard "1,2,3, Manners, Etiquette & Self-Esteem" for "U" and "M&E."

## Self-Esteem Success Tips

### Your Attitude

Success depends on your attitude. There is a saying, "Your attitude will determine your altitude."

- Stop blaming others for what is happening to "U" in your life.
- Start looking at what "U" can change for the life "U" want.
- Be responsible for your actions.
- When "U" do something wrong, don't point the finger at someone else.
- Don't give excuses.
- Don't say things like, "They started it", or "They told me to do it."

So, no more excuses. If "U" want to be successful, take responsibility for reaching your goals.

## How To Build Your Self-Esteem

- Surround yourself with happy people.
- Work with a purpose.
- Realize every day that life is a gift.
- Get up and get out, move your body.
- Give all "U" have to accomplish what "U" want.

- Discover new things like travel and education.
- Share your happiness and laughter with others.
- Believe in yourself.
- Do not live in the past.
- Always learn from your mistakes.

## How to Meet New People

When meeting new people, being polite and real are very important. Always introduce yourself. Say hello and state your name clearly. "U" should also say a little something about yourself and that you're pleased to meet them.

Also, when meeting new people, be prepared to discuss a few topics. These topics could be about your favorite media, books, games, current events, sports, hobbies, pets, etc. When in doubt, "U" can always make small talk about the weather.

## Making New Friends

Being polite and being yourself are the two biggest steps to remember when meeting new people. It was good for Manners to shake hands in the past, but today a fist bump will work.

When "U" see someone struggling with something, offer to help. "U" never know when someone might need an extra hand. Helping someone else shows "U" care about them. It's a great way to start new friendship.

## When to Speak

Listen before "U" speak; your words are important. Having your words heard is what "U" want. The key to being heard is first to listen. Let people finish what they are saying before "U" ask a question or attempt to give your answer or opinion. Once the individual sees "U" are interested in them, they might be more likely to listen to "U" when "U" are speaking.

## Solving A Problem

There is more than one way to solve a problem. If you're not open to listening, then "U" may limit your options and never solve the problem. Be open to listening.

Study the problem closely before "U" make a move to devote time and attention. This effort will guide "U" in the correct direction to solve the problem.

No matter what comes up and who "U" are dealing with remember:

- "U" know how to follow directions well.

- "U" are smart with a sharp mind.

- "U" can make good decisions and follow directions.

# When to Speak In A Public Place

## Make Sure You

- Are considerate.
- Don't disturb the people around "U".
- Keep your voice down (use your inside voice).

## Speak Up for Yourself

- It's time to speak up and say what "U" feel.
- Ask for what "U" need.
- Share your opinion.
- Tell others what "U" think.
- Let your wants be known, as no one can see your thoughts or know what you're thinking.
- Speak up clearly to be understood.

Mistakes can help "U" reclaim parts of yourself "U" forgot about. No one is perfect.

Negative self-talk damages your ability to function and limits your growth. "U" want the ability to have healthy Self-Esteem.

## When Emotions Arise or Feelings are Hurt

- Emotions between one person and another can arise because of a simple misunderstanding.
- Seek to reconcile differences and always try to resolve your differences by standing up for yourself.
- No one gets to go back in time. Look ahead to your future.

## Share with Others

Sharing with others is a way to give back what "U" have been given. We have a lot of things to share, like our opinions, ideas, things we have learned, and even our time. Will "U" share?

- The Material "M&E"

A longing to protect your body and your material things to have others notice them and look at them favorably but not take advantage of "U."

- The Social "M&E"

Recognition and even acceptance from other relationships that people will play a significant role in your identity.

- The Spiritual "M&E"

Feelings and emotions. Your innermost thoughts, desires, and dreams. The relationship with yourself and knowledge about yourself.

**Self-Respect** – the Pride and Confidence a person has in them self-behaving with Honor and Dignity.

**Self-Integrity** – strong morals and values. A person with self-integrity follows their principles in both their words and actions.

**Self Esteem** – the way a person has confidence in their worth or abilities.

- Self-Esteem serves as a protective function in life.
- Self-Esteem is our respect for others and maintaining a high regard for ourselves.
- Self-Esteem is a basic human need for motivation and success.

You're unique with a Special Gift. Learn to live to make the Best Life for "U."

## Broken Character

To stop the problem of broken character, surround yourself with positive people. "U" know the difference between right & wrong.

- Be "U" and Love Yourself.
- Don't despise people who hate themselves and consider themselves worthless and incapable of being Loved or showing Love.

## Make A "*BE*" Choice

Whenever you go out in public:

- Will "U" choose to "Be" patient?
- Will "U" choose to "Be" polite?
- Will "U" "Be" engaged with those around "U"?
- Will "U" "Be" your best?

## Consider Others

Please don't talk badly about others or disrespect them.

- Don't yell. Speak in a proper tone to sound and look respectful.
- When at school, greet others while using your inside voice— respect the personnel.

Now "U" must take the step to "BE" Make a choice and "BE" it!

## Setting Goals

Making Goals and having Big Dreams is terrific, but it will not just happen on your own. Most people realize they need a change in their lives.

Although the dictionary has a definition of success, only "U" can determine what it means to "U." If "U" want to be successful, it begins with a decision. You can have the best experiences, but it's not your life but your journey.

The goal of this book is to give "U" information that "U" can choose to help "U." So, take a tip from here and there. Flip the pages until "U" find what can assist your efforts. "U" have already read the Manners, Etiquette, and Self-Esteem information. They All work Together to Help "U" Reach your Goal(s) for Success.

## How to Develop Goals

- Think about your Goals.
- Write the Goals down.
- Determine whether they are Short-Term or Long-Term.
- Start on the Goals.
- Set a timeframe for completion.
- Check the direction of the Goal(s). Your Goals give "U" direction. Go back and check to see if "U" are doing what "U" said.
- Stay Focused on the Goal(s). The Goal is choosing the target to aim at, and once "U" know, "U" can line it up.

Always try to accomplish your Goals on time. Manage your time to avoid becoming overwhelmed. Pick one thing and get started. Don't give "UP" in the process. Be thankful "U" can work on your Goals.

## Dress For the Occasion

Different jobs and occasions may require varied attire. It's important to always dress for the occasion. If "U" need more clarification, always ask.

- In the workspace - remember that you're in a public space. Don't disturb the people around "U." Keep your voice down and never use foul language.

  Swearing is offensive. Choose words that respect others' ears.

- Doing the job - having a job is a huge responsibility. "U" have to show up on time and work hard, or "U" may only have a job for a short time.

- When preparing for school or a job for the next day be sure to get enough sleep.

- Always be attentive, helpful, polite, and courteous to your teachers, supervisors, customers, and coworkers. When "U" see someone struggling with something, offer to help them "U" never know when someone might need an extra hand. Helping someone else is an act that shows "U" care about them or the work.

- First, out of respect, if someone needs a seat, especially a pregnant lady, be courteous and stand. Also, be courteous to an elderly person whether disabled or not. This honors the individual with respect.

## Self-Esteem Communication Skills

Having effective communication skills is a must to maneuver in this virtual world.

- Internet – The Internet is a global computer network providing various information and communication facilities, consisting of interconnected networks.

When "U" don't see people or hear their voices, it is easy to forget good **Manners**.

- Cell phone conversations sometimes need to be held in a better place. Remember other people's space. Be considerate of the loudness of your voice when talking on the phone.
- Email is a popular and easy way to stay in touch. It is available to connect just as fast as your cell phone.
- Social media is often used to share information as well.

Always be cautious when using the internet. Keep your important information to yourself. Most of all, let your imagination have fun as "U" grow in the interconnected world.

## Building Success Skills

Success skills help open doors. You'll need them on your journey.

- Reading – Reading helps us learn and leads to our success. The key to reading is to get pleasure and enjoyment of reading for knowledge to succeed.
- Write – Writing moves thoughts from our minds onto paper. It is a way to express ourselves and to keep vital information that we can use now or later.
- Penmanship – Your signature is essential. Learn to write it in cursive, known as a script, not in block letters, be proud when "U" write your name.
- Social Security Number – It's crucial to learn your number for your use only; never give it out over the phone.
- Saving – Money is needed to live. Don't spend it all in one place. Learn to save for a rainy day.

There is much to learn about Self-Esteem and Success. The hope is that the content of this book will be beneficial to "U" as "U" move forward in life, building your Confidence and Character.

**Self Esteem** Is "**Forever**".

"**It's To The Point.**" Apply It To "**Your Life.**"

Make It **"Fit"** For **"U."**

# Virtues: The Gifts Within

Assertiveness

Caring

Cleanliness

Compassion

Confidence

Consideration

Courage

Courtesy

Creativity

Detachment

Determination

Enthusiasm

Excellence

Faithfulness

Flexibility

Forgiveness

Friendliness

Generosity

Gentleness

Helpfulness

Honesty

Honor

Humility

Idealism

Joyful

Justice

Kindness

Love

Loyalty

Mercy

Moderation

Modesty

Obedience

Orderliness

Patience

Peaceful

Prayerful

Purposeful

Reliability

Respect

Responsibility

Reverence

Self-discipline

Service

Steadfastness

Tact---

Thankful

Tolerance

Trust

Trustworthy

Truthful

Unity

The student creed reflects the principles of the five tenets – courtesy, integrity, perseverance, self-control, and indomitable spirit.

## STUDENT CREED

I must develop myself in a positive manner and avoid anything that will reduce my mental growth and physical health.

I must develop self-discipline in order to bring out the best in others.

I must use what I learn in class constructively and defensively to help myself and never be abusive to another.

Winners Never Quit!
Quitters Never Win!
I Choose To Be A Winner!

I truly appreciate you reading this book. I hope that prioritizing the "1,2,3, Manners, Etiquette, and Self-Esteem" will have the same effect on your life as mine. Resource pictures on the pages are designed to help you put this book's ideas into action and spark interesting conversations with others in your community, school, or neighborhood. Help them learn and remember the "1,2,3," and please stay in touch. I love hearing from readers. "U" can always email "M&E" at Manners.Etiquett@yahoo.com

# Índice

SEÑORA MODALES Y SEÑOR ETIQUETA

## Dedicatoria

Gracias a todos aquellos con los que he conectado durante este viaje. Me han ayudado a convertirme en la persona que soy hoy.

A mi esposo, por estar siempre detrás de mí al cien por ciento con el equipo de ALFRBA en cada desfile del Día del Bronx. A Jo's Printing por darnos el aspecto del 'BX' Bronx Love.

A mis maravillosos hermanos, Fredtrine Jefferies y Alfred Jefferies. Las dos primeras letras de nuestros nombres crearon el nombre del negocio familiar «ALFRBA» (pronunciado *al-fer-ba*).

A nuestra madre de tres hijos, una autodenominada "sureña". Kathreen Jefferies no se anduvo con rodeos. Ella me inculcó los modales, la etiqueta y la autoestima que ahora comparto con ustedes.

También quiero mencionar a mi hijo, Theodore *Teddy* Gibson, y a mi sobrino, Miles Brinson, que se han ido al cielo. Sus vidas fueron cortas y dulces. Toda su familia los extraña.

# Introducción

Algunos pueden decir que las palabras «Sí, señora» y «No, señor» están pasados de moda, pero la autora cree que los buenos modales son relevantes y necesarios en la actualidad.

En una época en la que es cada vez más frecuente salir a cenar fuera y pasar menos tiempo en casa en la mesa, este libro adquiere un significado especial. *Modales y Etiqueta* (*M&E*) *con autoestima* comparte tres estrategias (Modales, Etiqueta y Autoestima) para criar a nuestros hijos y convertirlos en personas exitosas y positivas. Este libro les ayudará a crecer durante todas las edades y etapas de su vida.

La experiencia de su autora compartiendo, enseñando y empoderando a sus alumnos la convierte en una persona especialmente capacitada para guiar a los padres a involucrar a sus hijos en la exploración del abecé de los modales, la etiqueta y la autoestima a través de la interacción en casa.

Este libro tiene como objetivo ayudar a los estudiantes a construir amistades, comunicarse y prosperar en la escuela, lo que puede potenciar el sentido de pertenencia con los demás. Queremos niños pacientes, amables, humildes, agradecidos y respetuosos, características que los ayudarán a desarrollar una buena ética laboral.

Un carácter fuerte y una imagen sana de sí mismos ayudan a los niños a crecer lo mejor posible. No se puede obligar a un niño a mostrar agradecimiento por todo, pero sí se puede criar a un niño exitoso y responsable que se convierta en un adulto que enorgullezca a sus padres.

Gracias por tomarse el tiempo de leer el primer libro bilingüe de (nombre del autor). Será una buena lectura para padres, profesores y alumnos.

La misión de este libro es llamar la atención sobre la necesidad de desarrollar habilidades para la vida y la autoestima.

En este libro se comparten ideas, se responden preguntas y se dan instrucciones sencillas para facilitar su aplicación en la vida.

La planificación cuidadosa dará sus frutos en el aprendizaje de las habilidades sociales, vitales y de autoestima. A medida que el mundo cambia a nuestro alrededor, el proceso sigue siendo el mismo de la A a la Z, enseñando habilidades como el «1,2,3» y creyendo que cada niño las necesita más hoy que ayer.

La organización de la autora, ALFRBA, trabaja para tratar y mejorar las habilidades sociales y cree que *M&E con Autoestima* es una necesidad para todos.

Cada tema de este libro amerita una profunda reflexión para el niño, pero es solo un punto de partida. Con la orientación adecuada, nuestros hijos aprenderán a mantenerse fuertes frente a los obstáculos mientras aprenden principios importantes y cómo desenvolverse.

La Sra. Barbara espera que priorizar el «1,2,3» de Modales y etiqueta con autoestima tenga el mismo efecto en su vida que el que ha tenido en la de ella.

Durante muchos años ha aconsejado y ejercido su oficio, creando y presentando varios talleres sobre *M&E con Autoestima*. Durante años, ha anhelado poner un libro como este en manos de los demás.

Estas páginas albergan una profunda sabiduría, pues la Sra. Barbara ha encontrado una hermosa forma de abrirse a los niños. ¿Qué puede ser mejor que divertirse tranquilamente con sus hijos y, al mismo tiempo, sentar las bases de su equilibrio social y emocional y de su éxito a medida que crecen?

Barbara cree que la mejor manera de ayudar a los niños es dotar a sus padres de conocimientos y habilidades sobre el desarrollo infantil para que tengan éxito durante su infancia y más allá.

Barbara ha enseñado modales, etiqueta y autoestima durante más de treinta años. Cree que los buenos modales son esenciales si una persona desea tener éxito. En su afán por conseguirlo, ha diseñado dos personajes de peluche con la forma de las letras M y E, su marca registrada. También ha creado servilletas que acompañan a los personajes de peluche, con palabras en español e inglés, para que los niños aprendan de una forma divertida.

Este encantador libro puede compartirse como lectura en voz alta con niños pequeños y como una forma de aprender dos idiomas al mismo tiempo. Así, son dos libros en uno, con secciones separadas en inglés y español.

ESTAS SON ALGUNAS EXPRESIONES
BILINGÜES UTILIZADAS PARA MOSTRAR
BUENOS MODALES

Yes
  Sí

Please
  Por Favor

You're Welcome
  DeNada

Excuse Me
  Perdónenme

Thank You
  Gracias

May I
  ¿Puedo...

I'm Sorry
  Lo Siento

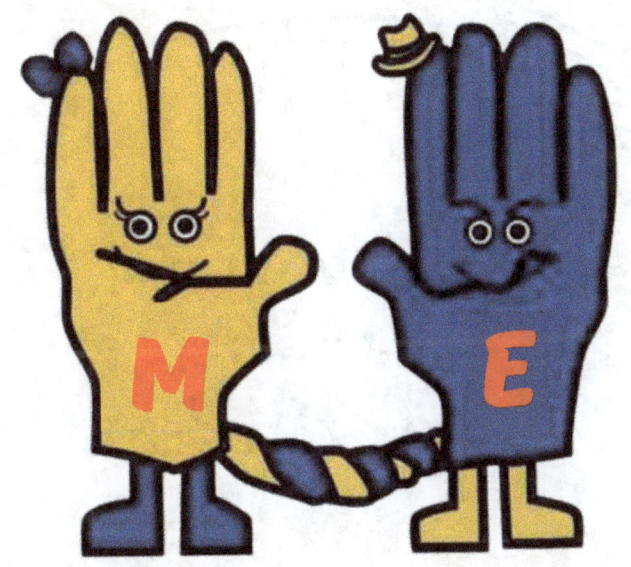

SEÑORA MODALES Y SEÑOR ETIQUETA

Es La Hora De Los Modales

# Compromiso de Modales y Etiqueta con Autoestima

Prometo usar mis *modales* todos los días.

A decir «Gracias», «De nada» y «Disculpe».

Me comprometo a decir «¿Cómo estás?» y

«¿Qué tal el día?».

Decir, «Buenos días», «Buenas tardes»

y «Buenas noches» a mis seres queridos.

Prometo ser educado. Decir «Lo siento» y acordarme de cuidar y

ser amable con mis amigos.

Prometo portarme bien y ser

respetuoso conmigo mismo y con los demás.

Prometo escuchar, seguir las instrucciones

y ser honesto.

Prometo usar mi *etiqueta* todos los días y

saludar a los demás con una sonrisa.

Prometo lavarme las manos antes y después de comer y usar la

servilleta. También colocar la mano sobre el regazo y el codo

fuera de la mesa.

Me comprometo a desarrollar mi *autoestima* cada día. Aprenderé a relacionarme con los demás y a convertirme en la mejor persona que pueda ser.

# La importancia de los modales

Los modales y la etiqueta (M&E) no son lo mismo. Los modales y la etiqueta son diferentes y no deben confundirse.

- Los modales son los comportamientos externos que reflejan la actitud de una persona en una interacción humana positiva.
- La etiqueta es una norma de conducta con reglas sociales relacionadas con la interacción conductual con los demás.

Los modales son habilidades para la vida que muestran cómo una persona se comporta con los demás. Muchas personas esperan y respetan los buenos modales. Cuando las personas exhiben buenos modales, hacen ver a quienes les rodean que respetan los sentimientos de los demás. Con buenos modales, es probable que fomentemos el buen comportamiento de los demás.

Sería prudente que los padres corrigieran la forma en que sus hijos les contestan a ellos y a los demás. Empiece la enseñanza pronto.

Vamos, equipo, tenemos trabajo que hacer. ¡Los buenos modales y la etiqueta son para siempre.

## Palabras para recordar

**Disculpe -** Puede utilizarse cuando es necesario llamar la atención de alguien, pasar por delante de alguien, pedir a alguien que repita lo que acaba de decir, o cuando alguien pasa por delante de otro y choca accidentalmente con él.

**Me permites –** Puede utilizarse para pedir permiso para hacer algo o ir a algún sitio.

**¿Puedo...?** – Se emplea para preguntar si puedes ayudar a alguien con algo. A los padres les gusta que los niños usen esta expresión cuando quieren hacer algo.

**Ser educado –** Tener o mostrar un comportamiento respetuoso y considerado con los demás. Al ser educados, los niños tienen la oportunidad de mostrar su respeto por los demás.

**Ser amable** – La amabilidad se basa en lo amistosa, generosa y considerada que es una persona con los demás.

**Ser ordenado** – Limpia lo que ensucies en casa y cuando visites a otras personas. Ayuda a mantener limpias las zonas públicas. Devuelve los objetos al lugar donde los encontraste.

**Compartir** – Compartir es el acto de tomar algo de lo que tienes (juguetes, comida, juegos) y dárselo a otro. Compartir con un amigo demuestra que no eres egoísta. Demuestra a los demás que te preocupas por ellos y por sus necesidades o deseos.

**Ser agradecido** – Expresar gratitud por lo que tienes. Estar agradecido por lo que posees y demostrárselo a los demás.

**Ser feliz** – Mostrar satisfacción con lo que se tiene. Nadie tiene el control total sobre la felicidad, pero tú puedes elegir trabajar cada día para ser más feliz.

# LOS MODALES SON PARA SIEMPRE

- Cortés
- Buen oyente
- Respetuoso
- Amable
- Educado
- Ordenado
- Puntual

- Por favor
- Disculpe
- Me permite
- Lo siento
- Gracias

# Modales cuando una puerta está cerrada

Haz lo siguiente antes de entrar en una habitación con la puerta cerrada.

- Respeta la privacidad de los demás.
- Llama primero a la puerta.
- Antes de abrir la puerta, asegúrate de que alguien te invita a entrar a la habitación.
- Puede que tengas que esperar a que la persona abra la puerta.

## Al salir de una habitación

- Nunca des portazos.
- Aprende a sujetar la puerta y a cerrarla suavemente.
- Es amable mantener la puerta abierta para los demás al entrar y salir de una habitación.

# Los modales son para siempre

Los modales, como tu corazón, te acompañan cada día. Recuerda lo importante que es pensar en los demás y pedir perdón inmediatamente si le haces algo malo a alguien, aunque sea un accidente.

## Modales en casa

Formar parte de una familia puede ser un trabajo difícil, pero es importante hablar siempre a la gente con un tono de voz respetuoso. Ya sea tu madre, tu padre, tu hermana o tu hermano, recuerda siempre la regla de oro de los modales, que dice: «Trata a los demás como quieres que te traten».

Algunas veces tendrás que dar un poco para recibir un poco. Lo importante es ser siempre lo más educado y comprensivo posible.

## La paciencia es una virtud

Este comportamiento demuestra un alto nivel moral. La paciencia es la capacidad de esperar algo sin enfadarse ni alterarse; es una cualidad excelente en una persona. La paciencia, la amabilidad y el autocontrol ayudan a las personas a ser mejores versiones de sí mismas.

## Hacer tus tareas

Puede que estés a cargo de las tareas de la casa, como limpiar tu habitación, fregar los platos, etc. Mantenerte al día con tus tareas es crucial. Si no haces tus tareas a tiempo, te estás creando más trabajo. Puedes acabar haciendo el doble de trabajo si no lo haces bien a la primera.

## Trabajo voluntario

Haz que cada día cuente y difunde el amor. Utiliza tus habilidades para ayudar a los demás. Entrega parte de tu tiempo ayudando en tu comunidad, sin esperar nada a cambio.

## Sonríe

Si te invito a mirarte en un espejo para ver tu sonrisa, ¿te sonreirías a ti mismo?

Intenta sonreír a un transeúnte. Cuando sonríes, la persona puede ver cómo te sientes. No te imaginas lo mucho que una sonrisa puede cambiar la perspectiva de alguien. Con una sonrisa sincera puedes hacer que el peor día de alguien sea mejor.

Recuerda que una sonrisa puede mejorar el día de esa persona. Incluso puede hacer que esa persona te devuelva la sonrisa a ti o a alguien más, causando un efecto dominó de felicidad.

Puedes hacer un cumplido, felicitar o elogiar a alguien por algo que haya hecho con una sonrisa. Las sonrisas y los cumplidos se llevan muy bien. Puedes hacer que alguien se sienta bien consigo mismo y apreciado por ti.

## Aprende a tocar

Hay muchas formas de tocar a los demás, como abrazarse o tomarse de la mano. También puedes tocar a alguien con un pulgar hacia arriba, palabras de ánimo o una sonrisa. Estas son formas de tocar a los demás amablemente.

## Todos pueden aprender

Debes estar abierto a aprender. Haz preguntas y escucha sus respuestas. Cuando la gente responda a tus preguntas, ten paciencia y no los interrumpas. Espera a que terminen y contesta.

## Ceder un asiento

Si estás sentado y te das cuenta de que una mujer embarazada, una persona mayor o una persona discapacitada necesita un asiento, permíteles que tomen el tuyo. Esta pequeña acción demuestra mucho respeto y reverencia.

Asegúrate de dedicar tiempo a cada tema, (modales, etiqueta y autoestima), para que recibas toda la información que necesitas. No hay límite para lo que puedes aprender con la práctica.

It's Manners & Etiquette Time..........

"Ms. Manners Meets Mr. Etiquette"

M is for Manners    E is for Etiquette

For You And

"Manners & Etiquette"

Are Forever

# Modales y etiqueta

Los modales y la etiqueta van de la mano.

Cuando das las gracias, eso son modales.

Cuando utilizas el tenedor y el cuchillo en lugar de las manos, eso es etiqueta en la mesa.

Ahora ves cómo los modales y la etiqueta pueden ir de la mano.

Recuerda siempre a las personas que te han ayudado en el camino. No te olvides de ayudar a los demás.

# Recordatorios de buenos modales

- Ser maleducado es inaceptable. Si hay una persona maleducada cerca, intenta alejarte de su presencia.

- Sé puntual. Si dices que vas a estar en un sitio, la gente espera que estés allí. Haz lo que dijiste que harías.

- No te burles de los demás. Recuerda jugar y divertirte, pero no te burles de los demás. No te burles de ellos ni hagas bromas sobre ellos para molestarlos.

- Respétate a ti mismo y a los demás. Recuerda que las palabras que utilizas pueden volver y hacerte daño a ti también.

- Nada de lenguaje soez. Las palabras ofensivas como insultar, maldecir o hacer comentarios groseros son inaceptables.

## *Bullying*, burlas y más...

El *bullying* NO es una broma.

¿M&E oíste?

El *bullying* NO es una broma.

Soy un chico que conoce a una chica, y el acoso no es una broma

ni para ella ni para mí.

No es ninguna broma para ella o para mí.

Ambos sabemos cómo se siente, así que escúchanos.

Es real.

Respeta a tu amigo y también a los demás.

El *bullying* duele, y a ti te puede dañar.

El *bullying* puede ocurrir en la escuela, fuera de ella,

e incluso en casa.

El *ciberbullying* o acoso *online* también es malo.

¿M&E oíste? El *bullying* NO es ninguna broma.

Recuerda respetar a tus amigos y a los demás.

No querrás que las faltas de respeto vuelvan y

te dañen a ti también.

¿M&E oíste?

El bullying NO es una broma.


Los modales son para siempre. Es de buena educación seguir la etiqueta adecuada. Es un principio de vida. Estás listo.

**«*Los modales son importantes. Úsalos*».** RESPETO.

SEÑORA MODALES Y SEÑOR ETIQUETA

Es La Hora De La Etiqueta

# La importancia de la etiqueta

La etiqueta es el código de conducta habitual en la sociedad o entre los miembros de una profesión o grupo determinado.

En la actualidad, las normas de etiqueta cambian y se suelen solapar en nuestra sociedad. Ya sea en casa o en un entorno público, la etiqueta refleja nuestra conducta, nuestro valor y nuestro respeto por los demás. Muestra nuestras habilidades para la vida.

En un entorno social, es importante respetarse a uno mismo y a los demás en la mesa.

## Poner la mesa

Cuando te sientes a la mesa para cenar, podrás saber qué tipo de comida se está sirviendo por la forma en que la mesa está arreglada. También sabrás qué utensilios utilizar y la forma correcta de hacerlo. Es posible que veas uno, dos o tres tenedores a la izquierda del plato. La colocación de los cubiertos comienza desde el exterior hacia el interior del plato.

Al mirar la colocación de los cubiertos, ¿qué tenedor está en el exterior? Los utilizarás de afuera hacia adentro. Si el tenedor más pequeño para ensalada está en el exterior, se te servirá la ensalada antes del plato principal. Si el tenedor de ensalada está en el interior, el plato principal será el primero.

De cualquier forma, la etiqueta básica respecto a los cubiertos es siempre la misma, independientemente del número de utensilios o de lo elegante que sea la vajilla: empezar de fuera hacia dentro con cada plato.

Este es un recordatorio amistoso sobre modales y etiqueta en la mesa. Recuerda lo siguiente.

## Sé puntual cuando te inviten a cenar

- Es fundamental ser siempre puntual; llegar tarde no es de buena educación. Empieza a arreglarte un poco antes para llegar a tiempo.
- La etiqueta es algo más que saber qué cubiertos utilizar.
- El verdadero propósito de la etiqueta es siempre mostrar respeto y amabilidad.
- Para los niños en un entorno escolar, la etiqueta empieza en la puerta y continúa en las mesas cuando se sientan con los demás.

## Comidas al estilo familiar

Cuando sea el momento de sentarse a comer, saca tu silla con cuidado (entra por la izquierda y sal por la derecha). Asegúrate de acercar tu silla a la mesa por si otros tienen que pasar por detrás de ti.

El orden en la mesa es clave. Hay un plato delante de cada persona. La comida debe pasarse en el sentido contrario a las agujas del reloj, es decir, hacia tu derecha. Pasa todos los platos en la misma dirección. Para empezar, pasa la comida a tu derecha. Sujeta el recipiente para la persona de tu derecha y pásalo. Si eres el primero, sírvete un poco, luego empieza a pasar pero pregunta a la persona de tu izquierda si quiere algo. Si dice que sí, sírvele primero, no a ti.

Evita pasar por encima de alguien para tomar un plato. Si quieres algo de la mesa, sé educado y pídele a alguien que te haga el favor de pasar. Siempre recuerda dar las gracias a la persona que te entrega el plato.

## Cena sencilla o elegante

Cuando te sientes, fíjate en el entorno. En un entorno formal, habrá platos de carga o platos de servicio, que son platos grandes puestos debajo del plato de la cena. Los platos de servicio mantienen limpio el mantel. Se mantienen durante toda la comida.

## Observa la mesa

En la mesa, es posible que veas una servilleta de colores en uno de los vasos y tal vez algunas velas. Esto es lo que constituye una mesa bonita. También verás los cubiertos sobre la mesa. Recuerda utilizar los cubiertos desde afuera hacia adentro. Los cubiertos no deben tocar la mesa. Después de comer, los cubiertos se quedan en el plato. El camarero retirará los cubiertos una vez terminada la comida.

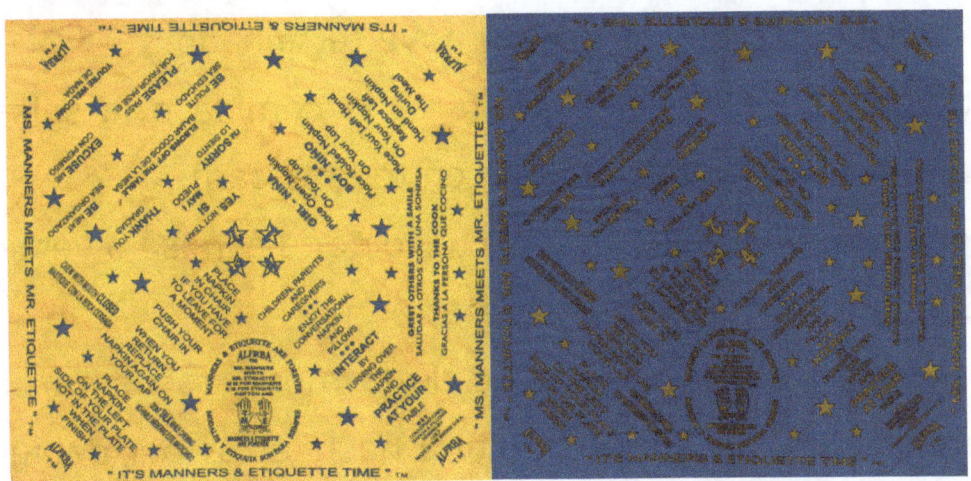

## La servilleta

Es apropiado poner la servilleta sobre tu regazo tan pronto como la recibas, utilizando tu mano izquierda. Permanecerá allí durante toda la comida, y solo puedes utilizarla para mantener tu boca limpia.

- Las servilletas para chicas deben abrirse completamente.
- Las servilletas para chicos se doblan por la mitad.
- La servilleta permanece en el regazo – nunca la coloques en la mesa hasta que la comida haya terminado.
- Utiliza la servilleta para quitarte la comida o la salsa de la boca. No utilices la servilleta en toda la cara.
- Mete la servilleta dentro del cuello de tu camisa o vestido solo cuando comas marisco o pasta.
- Al levantarte temporalmente de la mesa, recuerda poner la servilleta en la silla y empujarla hacia atrás por debajo de la mesa.

- Cuando vuelvas a tu asiento, volverás a poner la servilleta sobre el regazo.

- Recuerda sentarte siempre erguido y nunca hundido en la silla.

- Al terminar la cena, coloca la servilleta en el lado izquierdo de tu plato, luego levántate y empuja tu silla debajo de la mesa. Así el personal sabrá que terminaste de comer.

## Vasos

Tanto en las mesas elegantes como en las sencillas, siempre habrá tres vasos por servicio. Uno para el agua, otro para el vino tinto y otro para el vino blanco. Es posible que no se utilicen, pero ésta es la disposición estándar de los vasos y copas en la mesa. Las copas flauta se utilizan para el vino espumoso.

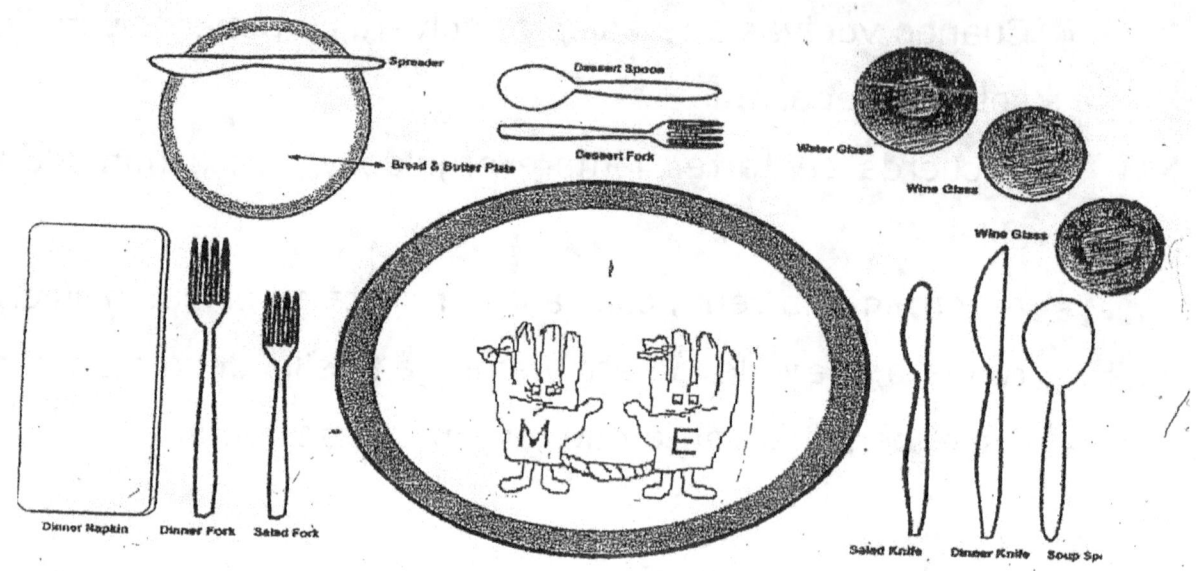

## Pan y mantequilla

Comparte la mantequillera.

- Pon la mantequilla en tu plato y utiliza un cuchillo para mantequilla.

- En la panera suele caber una ración por persona.

- Asegúrate de tocar solo tu ración.

- Parte el pan (no lo cortes) en un trozo del tamaño de un bocado por vez.

- Es fundamental tomar un segundo trozo de pan solo después de asegurarse de que todos hayan tenido la oportunidad de tomar su primer trozo.

## Saleros y pimenteros

- El salero y el pimentero deben pasarse juntos, aunque el comensal solo haya pedido uno.

## Etiqueta para la sopa

- La sopa debe tomarse con cuchara. Al sacar la cuchara de la sopa desde el lado del tazón o plato de sopa más alejado de ti, toca suavemente con la parte inferior de la cuchara el borde del tazón.
- Cuando termines de comer, apoya siempre la cuchara en el plato que está debajo del tazón, no en el tazón. Así evitarás derramar sopa sobre la ropa.

- Los padres deben practicar junto con sus hijos la rutina de la sopa. Una vez aprendida, se sentirán cómodos con este método para comer.

## Sopa asiática

- En algunas comunidades asiáticas, es normal relamerse los labios al comer. También es normal sorber fideos o sopas. En EE.UU., hacer ruidos al comer es considerado de mala educación. Para estos asiáticos, suele ser educado sorber o hacer ruidos al comer. Se considera mejor cuando se disfruta sonoramente. Para los asiáticos, es una señal de agradecimiento al cocinero. Adapta tu forma de comer a la zona, restaurante u hogar en el que te encuentres.

## No mojar dos veces

- Nunca mojes un alimento en una salsa, tomes un bocado y luego lo vuelvas a mojar.
- Sumerge en la salsa solo los trozos que no hayas comido.

## Rezar antes de comer

En algunas cenas, se puede recitar una oración de agradecimiento. El anfitrión puede optar por recitar también una oración antes de comer. Incluso es posible que te pidan que hagas la oración. Si no te sientes cómodo haciéndolo, puedes negarte educadamente.

## En la mesa

Saluda a los demás con una sonrisa. También está bien conversar un poco.

- Sé respetuoso y amable. Respétate siempre a ti mismo y a los demás.
- Siéntate para disfrutar de una buena comida y conversación.
- Mantén los codos fuera de la mesa.
- En un entorno familiar, puede ser aceptable apoyar los codos en la mesa. Observa lo que hace el anfitrión.

## Comiendo tu comida

- Inclínate ligeramente sobre el plato mientras comes para que la comida que se derrame caiga sobre el plato y no sobre tu regazo.
- Debes masticar con la boca cerrada. Masticar con la boca abierta no es de buena educación.
- Nunca hables mientras masticas.
- No juegues ni cantes en la mesa.

## Cómo cortar los alimentos

Si existe la posibilidad de que tengas que cortarlos en trozos del tamaño de un bocado, sujetar bien el cuchillo y el tenedor te dará mayor control sobre la comida de tu plato.

## Recordatorio del cuchillo

- Durante la comida, el filo debe estar orientado hacia el plato.
- Pasa el tenedor a la mano derecha con los dientes hacia arriba.

- Sostén el cuchillo con la mano izquierda y empuja la comida hacia el tenedor. El cuchillo también es necesario para ayudar a colocar los bocados en el tenedor. Está bien utilizar un tenedor sin cuchillo.

## Etiqueta en diferentes entornos culturales

Puede que te encuentres en una situación en la que la comida que te sirvan sea totalmente nueva para ti. Muchos alimentos, especias y hierbas son gustos adquiridos, así que no te sorprendas si no te gusta todo. Puede que la comida china sea tu favorita, pero ¿qué te parece el sushi? La comida *soul*, española, jamaicana, africana, india, italiana o de Medio Oriente también son opciones. ¡Hay tantos tipos de comida en nuestro mundo! He aquí algunas cosas que debes recordar cuando pruebas alimentos nuevos.

- Abstenerse de criticar la comida.
- Es de buena educación probar al menos un poco de todo.
- Ten cuidado de no reaccionar mal si alguien te dice: «Oh, eso es una anguila», si no has comido anguila antes. No debes

decir: «¡Ugh!» En lugar de eso, di: «No, gracias». Se cortés y di: «Probaré otro plato».

## Comiendo espaguetis

- Gira los fideos alrededor del tenedor. A continuación, corta los espaguetis en porciones del tamaño de un bocado.

## Comiendo langosta y pinzas

- Ponte un babero o cuélgate una servilleta del cuello.
- Puedes utilizar el tenedor pequeño para sacar la carne de las pinzas.

## Para la carne grasa

A veces la comida puede tener grasa y/o cartílago, que puede ser difícil de masticar. Lleva la servilleta a la boca y pon la carne en la servilleta. A continuación, coloca el alimento en el borde del plato.

## Los dos estilos de cuchillos

Continental y europeo

- Continental

- Estilo de descanso y terminado

¿Te has preguntado cómo colocar los cubiertos en la mesa o en el plato? ¿Hay que cruzarlos o colocarlos a un lado del plato, o deben mantenerse con el filo hacia arriba?

La forma de poner los cubiertos en el plato determina si estás pidiendo más comida o diciendo que has terminado de comer.

## Estilo continental

La posición para comer al estilo continental es con las puntas del tenedor y el filo del cuchillo hacia abajo.

Descansar vs terminar

- Terminé.

- Manteniendo los cubiertos paralelos entre sí.

Continental
Resting Position

Continental
Finished Position

## Estilo americano

En la comida al estilo americano, coloca el tenedor hacia abajo. Este es el orden en el que uno de estos estilos aparece en el plato. El estilo americano (aunque las puntas deben estar hacia abajo), o puedes colocar las puntas del tenedor hacia abajo de manera que formen una X.

- Estilo americano
- Estilo de descanso y terminado

**American Resting Position**

**American Finished Position**

El método americano empieza igual que el continental. Sin embargo, la diferencia es que cuando hayas terminado de cortar la carne, pones tu cuchillo hacia abajo en la parte superior del plato con la hoja hacia el centro.

Si cenas al estilo americano, coloca el cuchillo justo cuando hayas terminado de comer. Las puntas del tenedor pueden estar arriba o abajo, junto al borde izquierdo del cuchillo.

## Terminar la comida

- Posición de descanso americana

American
Resting Position

- Posición de descanso continental

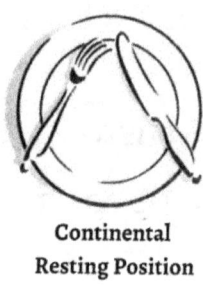

Continental
Resting Position

Existe un debate en torno a si hay que acabarse o no toda la comida del plato. Come lo que puedas, y nunca comas en exceso. Si tienes suficiente hambre, ¡no dudes en dejar limpio tu plato! *Bon Appétit!*

**Fin de la cena**

- El postre se sirve al final de la cena.

  - ○ Se retiran los platos.

  - ○ El postre puede servirse en otro ambiente más relajado.

**Recuerda lo siguiente:**

- La práctica hace la perfección.

- Invita a un amigo y empieza a practicar en casa para preparar tu próxima cena elegante o sencilla con un toque personal.

- Llega y sal a tiempo.

- Sé ordenado y limpia lo que ensucies.

- Aplaude al camarero o al cocinero por la comida.

- Los aplausos tienen lugar al final de la comida, cuando puedes aplaudir como expresión de aprobación, igual que se hace al terminar una actuación. Intenta prestar atención y estar en sintonía con quienes te rodean.

- Al salir de la comida, da las gracias al cocinero o al anfitrión.

- Las notas de agradecimiento son siempre bienvenidas.

- Recuerda que se aplican los modales, la cortesía y la regla de oro.

Los modales y la etiqueta van juntos como dos manos.Aquí estánel Sr. Modales y la Sra. Etiqueta.

It's Manners & Etiquette Time.........

"Ms. Manners Meets Mr. Etiquette"

M is for Manners    E is for Etiquette

For You And

"Manners & Etiquette"

Are Forever

Esta es la imagen original de este tema antes de que se añadiera la autoestima al flujo del programa.

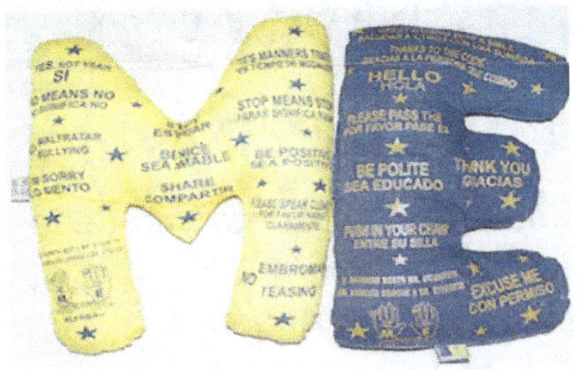

La regla de oro, que a menudo enseñan padres y profesores, es la siguiente: «Trata a los demás como te gustaría que te trten». ¿Cómo es posible? Recuerda siempre:

- Ser amable.

- Ser generoso.

- Ser considerado.

Lleva siempre contigo tus modales y etiqueta.

Se solapan entre sí de muchas maneras.

La información compartida te guiará

Es clara y va al grano.

Estás listo.

Los modales y la etiqueta van de la mano.

*Bon Appétit!*

SEÑORA MODALES Y SEÑOR ETIQUETA

Es La Hora
De La
Autoestima

# AUTOESTIMA

Es hora de cambiar tu comportamiento.

Tú puedes elegir.

¡Confía en ti mismo!

Afronta tus errores.

Aprende de tus errores.

Sueña a lo grande.

Fíjate metas.

Persigue tus deseos.

¡Dalo todo!

# La importancia de la autoestima

## «¡Cree en ti!»

Tienes la capacidad de creer en ti mismo. Puedes superar el dudar de ti y ganar confianza para actuar y hacer las cosas. Date cuenta de que puede que no todo te salga bien, pero tú puedes trabajar para lograr algo diferente. Valórate.

- La autoestima nos permite creer en nuestras capacidades y nos da la motivación para llevarlas a cabo y alcanzar una perspectiva positiva.
- La autoestima es el valor que nos damos a nosotros mismos.
- La autoestima es una necesidad humana básica para la motivación y para construir el éxito.
- La autoestima nos ayuda a ganar y mantener un gran concepto de nosotros mismos.
- La autoestima cumple una función protectora a lo largo de toda la vida.

Existen varios tipos de autoestima, pero no todas son iguales.

## Tres tipos de autoestima

1. **Autoestima alta** – Las personas con esta clase de autoestima tienden a aceptarse a sí mismas y a sus capacidades con confianza. Están dispuestas a dar y recibir cumplidos. Creen en su propio valor o capacidad.

2. **Autoestima inflada** – Las personas con autoestima inflada tienden a creerse mejor que los demás y siempre están dispuestas a subestimarlos. Su comportamiento puede ser negativo, sobre todo cuando hacen lo que sea para adelantarse a los demás. No suelen entablar relaciones significativas y sanas.

3. **Autoestima baja** – Las personas con el autoestima baja pueden ser demasiado críticas y no gustarse a sí mismas. Tienden a pensar que los demás son mejores que ellos, y

hacen bromas negativas sobre ellos mismos. Suelen ignorar sus propios logros.

Cada persona debe aprender a quererse a sí misma. Debes saber que tú eres alguien valioso y que puedes hacer todo lo que te propongas. En este proceso es importante saber:

- ¿Por qué existes?
- Saber hacia dónde te diriges.
- Estar dispuesto a aprender de tus errores.
- Dejar de huir del pasado.
- Tener la voluntad de hacer nuevos amigos.
- Mantener la fe y confiar en ti mismo en el proceso.
- Aprender a centrarte en hacer las cosas mejor y ser mejor.
- Seguir adelante, mantenerte fuerte y tener un objetivo.
- Completar lo que te propones.

Tienes que hablarte a ti mismo y decirte:

- Tengo confianza.

- Soy digno.
- Soy valioso.
- Soy fuerte.
- Soy amado.

En el proceso de desarrollo de la autoestima, aprenderás lo siguiente:

- La autoestima es el sentimiento interno de pertenencia, de ser lo suficientemente bueno y merecedor del amor de los demás.
- La autoestima es el acto de respetarse a uno mismo. No se puede esperar de los demás lo que no estás dispuesto a darte a ti mismo.
- Respetarse a sí mismo es tener orgullo y honrarse a sí mismo.
- Integridad es tener una moral o unos valores sólidos y seguir esos principios en lo que dices y en tus acciones.

Las personas, especialmente los niños, deben conocer el significado de la autoestima. Comparte con ellos formas para mejorar donde lo necesiten. Se debe enseñar a los niños:

- Lo que está bien y lo que está mal y una buena moral.
- Cómo elegir amigos positivos que los animen y no los derriben.
- Que pueden decir que no y no seguir el comportamiento de los demás.
- A celebrar con los demás cuando les ocurren cosas buenas.

**Modelo positivo de conducta**

Todos necesitan a alguien a quien admirar. Un modelo positivo inspira a los demás a vivir una vida con sentido. Son un ejemplo positivo de cómo:

- Vivir con integridad.
- Ser optimista.
- Tener esperanza.

- Tener determinación.

- Tener compasión.

- Exigir mucho de ti mismo y de tu trabajo.

- Dar un buen ejemplo

¡Tú también puedes ser un modelo a seguir!

Sin normas en nuestras vidas, todo estaría fuera de control. Las normas se establecen para servir de regla o guía. Hay que desarrollar normas, como modales, etiqueta y autoestima. Prueba nuestra norma «1,2,3 modales, etiqueta y autoestima para todos».

## Autoestima: consejos para triunfar

### Tu actitud

Hay un dicho que reza: «Tu actitud determinará tu altitud». El éxito depende de tu actitud.

- Deja de culpar a los demás de lo que ocurre en tu vida.

- Empieza a ver lo que puedes cambiar para tener la vida que deseas.

- Sé responsable de sus actos.

- Cuando hagas algo mal, no señales a otra persona.

- No pongas excusas.

- No digas cosas como «Ellos empezaron» o «Ellos me dijeron que lo hiciera».

Así que no más excusas. Si quieres tener éxito, asume la responsabilidad de alcanzar tus objetivos.

## Cómo fortalecer la autoestima

- Rodéate de gente feliz.

- Trabaja con un propósito.

- Ten en mente cada día que la vida es un regalo.

- Levántate y sal, mueve el cuerpo.

- Da todo lo que tengas para conseguir lo que quieres.

- Descubre cosas nuevas, como los viajes y la educación.

- Comparte tu felicidad y tu risa con los demás.

- Cree en ti.

- No vivas en el pasado.

- Aprende siempre de tus errores.

## Cómo conocer gente nueva

Al conocer gente nueva, ser educado y realista es muy importante. Preséntate siempre. Saluda y di tu nombre claramente. También debes decir algo sobre ti y que estás encantado de conocerlos.

Además, cuando conozcas a gente nueva, prepárate para tener algunos temas de conversación. Estos temas pueden ser sobre tus películas favoritas, libros, juegos, temas de actualidad, deportes, hobbies, mascotas, etc. En caso de duda, siempre puedes hablar un poco sobre el clima.

## Haciendo nuevos amigos

Al conocer gente nueva, los dos pasos más importantes que debes recordar son ser educado y ser tú mismo. Preséntate con un

«Hola» y di claramente tu nombre. Antes era de buena educación dar la mano, pero hoy basta con chocar los puños.

Cuando veas que alguien tiene dificultades con algo, ofrécele tu ayuda. Nunca se sabe cuándo alguien puede necesitar una mano extra. Ayudar a otra persona demuestra que los demás te importan. Es una forma estupenda de hacer nuevas amistades.

## Cuándo hablar

Escucha antes de hablar, tus palabras son importantes. Quieres ser escuchado. La clave para que te escuchen es escuchar primero. Deja que la gente termine lo que está diciendo antes de intervenir u opinar. Cuando la otra persona vea tu interés en lo que dice, estará más dispuesta a escucharte cuando hables.

## Resolver un problema

Hay más de una forma de resolver un problema. Si no estás abierto a escuchar, entonces podrías estar limitando tus opciones y no resolver nunca el problema. Debes estar dispuesto a escuchar.

Estudia el problema detenidamente antes de dedicarle tiempo y atención. Este esfuerzo te guiará en la dirección correcta para resolver el problema.

No importa lo que surja ni con quién tengas que tratar. Siempre recuerda:

- Sabes seguir bien las instrucciones.

- Eres inteligente y tienes una mente ágil.

- Puedes tomar buenas decisiones y seguir instrucciones.

## Cuándo hablar

### En un lugar público

- Sé considerado.
- No molestes a las personas a tu alrededor.
- Baja la voz.

### Expresa lo que piensas

- Es hora de hablar y decir lo que sientes.
- Pide lo que necesites.

- Comparte tu opinión.

- Dile a los demás lo que piensas.

- Di lo que necesitas, pues nadie puede ver ni leer tus pensamientos.

- Habla claro para que te entiendan.

Los errores pueden ayudarte a reivindicar partes de ti mismo que habías olvidado. Nadie es perfecto.

El pensamiento negativo sobre uno mismo daña la capacidad de funcionar y limita el crecimiento. Queremos la capacidad de tener una autoestima sana.

**Cuando surgen emociones o se hieren sentimientos**

- A veces pueden surgir emociones entre dos personas por un simple malentendido.

- Procura conciliar las diferencias e intenta resolverlas siempre expresando cómo te sientes.

- Nadie puede retroceder en el tiempo. Mira hacia adelante, hacia tu futuro.

## Comparte con otros

Compartir con otros es una forma de devolver lo que se nos ha dado. Tenemos muchas cosas que compartir, como nuestras opiniones, ideas, cosas que hemos aprendido e incluso nuestro tiempo. ¿Quieres compartir?

- M&E material

Un anhelo de proteger tu cuerpo y tus cosas materiales para que otros se fijen en ellos y los miren de manera favorable, pero no se aprovechen de ti.

- M&E social

Reconocimiento e incluso aceptación de que otras personas desempeñarán un papel importante en tu identidad.

- M&E espiritual

Sentimientos y emociones. Los pensamientos, deseos y sueños más íntimos. La relación con uno mismo y el conocimiento de uno mismo.

**Respeto por uno mismo** – el orgullo y la confianza que una persona tiene en sí misma comportándose con honor y dignidad.

**Integridad** – una moral y unos valores sólidos. Una persona íntegra sigue sus principios tanto en sus palabras como en sus acciones.

**Autoestima** – la confianza que una persona tiene en su valor o sus capacidades.

- La autoestima cumple una función protectora en la vida.
- La autoestima es el respeto que tenemos por los demás y la opinión que mantenemos sobre nosotros mismos.
- La autoestima es una necesidad humana básica para la motivación y el éxito.

Eres único con un don especial. Aprende a vivir para lograr tener una mejor vida.

### *Salirse de personaje*

Para acabar con el problema de ser inconsistente y *salirte de personaje*, rodéate de gente positiva. Conoce la diferencia entre el bien y el mal.

- Sé tú mismo y quiérete.
- No desprecies a las personas que se odian a sí mismas y se consideran inútiles e incapaces de ser amadas o de mostrar amor.

### Elige «Ser»

Cada vez que salgas en público:

- ¿Elegirás *ser* paciente?
- ¿Elegirás *ser* educado?
- ¿Te comprometerás con los que le rodean?
- ¿Serás tu mejor versión?

### Sé considerado con los demás

Por favor, no hables mal de los demás ni les faltes el respeto.

- No grites. Habla en un tono adecuado para parecer y sonar respetuoso.

- Cuando estés en la escuela, saluda a los demás en voz baja: respeta al personal.

Ahora debes dar el paso de SER ¡Elige SER!

**Fijar objetivos**

Fijarse objetivos y tener grandes sueños es estupendo, pero no sucederá por sí solo. La mayoría de las personas se da cuenta de que necesita un cambio en su vida para conseguirlos.

Aunque el diccionario tiene una definición de éxito, solo tú puedes determinar lo que significa para ti. Si deseas tener éxito, comienza con una decisión. Puedes escuchar las mejores experiencias de los demás, pero no se trata de tu vida, sino de tu viaje.

El objetivo de este libro es darte información que puedas elegir para ayudarte. Siéntete libre de tomar consejos de aquí y allá. Hojea las páginas hasta que encuentres lo que puede ayudar a tus esfuerzos. Ya leíste la información sobre modales, etiqueta y autoestima: todos ellos trabajan juntos para ayudarte a alcanzar el éxito.

## Cómo fijarte objetivos

- Piensa en tus objetivos.
- Escríbelos.
- Determina si son a corto o a largo plazo.
- Empieza por trabajar en los objetivos.
- Fija un plazo para alcanzarlos.
- Asegúrate de que vas en la dirección de los objetivos. Tus objetivos te guían. Si lo necesitas, vuelve a tus hoja de objetivos y comprueba si estás haciendo lo que dijiste.
- Mantente centrado en el(los) objetivo(s). El objetivo es elegir la diana a la que apuntar, y una vez que sepas cuál es, podrás alinearte con ella.

Intenta siempre cumplir tus objetivos puntualmente. Gestiona tu tiempo para no agobiarte. Elige algo y ponte manos a la obra.

Durante el proceso, no te rindas. Agradece que puedes trabajar en tus objetivos.

## Vístete para la ocasión

Diferentes trabajos y ocasiones pueden requerir atuendos distintos. Es importante vestirse siempre para la ocasión. Si necesitas aclarar algo, no dudes en preguntar.

• En el espacio de trabajo: recuerda que estás en un espacio público. No molestes a las personas que están a tu alrededor. Baja la voz y nunca utilices un lenguaje soez.

Decir palabrotas es ofensivo. Elige palabras respetuosas con los oídos de los demás.

• Haz el trabajo: tener un trabajo es una gran responsabilidad. Tienes que llegar a tiempo y trabajar duro, o puede que lo tengas por poco tiempo.

• Asegúrate de dormir lo suficiente cuando te prepares para el colegio o el trabajo del día siguiente.

- Sé siempre atento, servicial, educado y cortés con tus profesores, supervisores, clientes y compañeros de trabajo. Cuando veas que alguien tiene problemas con algo, ofrécele tu ayuda: nunca se sabe cuándo alguien puede necesitar una mano extra. Ayudar a los demás es un acto que demuestra tu interés por ellos y por tu trabajo.

- En primer lugar, por respeto, si alguien necesita sentarse, especialmente una mujer embarazada, sé cortés y ponte de pie. Del mismo modo, sé cortés con una persona mayor, discapacitada o no. Esto honra al individuo con respeto.

## Habilidades de comunicación y autoestima

Tener habilidades de comunicación efectivas es indispensable para maniobrar en este mundo virtual.

- Internet – Internet es una red informática mundial que ofrece una amplia variedad de servicios de información y comunicación y está formada por redes interconectadas.

151

Cuando no ves a la gente ni oyes sus voces, es fácil olvidar los buenos modales.

- A veces, las conversaciones por teléfono celular deben llevarse a cabo en un lugar apropiado. Recuerda respetar el espacio de los demás y ten en cuenta el volumen de tu voz cuando hables por teléfono.
- El correo electrónico es una vía popular y sencilla de mantenerse en contacto. Está disponible para conectarse tan rápido como el teléfono móvil.
- Las redes sociales también se utilizan a menudo para compartir información.

Sé siempre precavido cuando utilices internet. Guárdate la información importante para ti. Sobre todo, deja que tu imaginación se divierta mientras creces en el mundo interconectado

# Desarrollo de habilidades para el éxito

Las habilidades para el éxito ayudan a abrir puertas. Las necesitarás en tu viaje.

- Lectura – Leer nos ayuda a aprender y nos encamina hacia el éxito. La clave de la lectura es leer por placer y disfrute, o leer para aprender y alcanzar el éxito.

- Escritura – Escribir transporta los pensamientos de nuestra mente al papel. Es una forma de expresarnos y de guardar información vital que podemos utilizar en el momento o más adelante.

- Caligrafía – Tu firma es esencial. Aprende a escribirla en cursiva, lo que se conoce como letra de molde, no en imprenta. Siéntete orgulloso al escribir tu nombre.

- Número de la Seguridad Social – Es crucial que aprendas tu número solo para tu uso; nunca lo des por teléfono.

- Ahorrar – El dinero es necesario para vivir. No lo gastes todo en el mismo sitio. Aprende a ahorrar para los momentos difíciles.

Hay mucho que aprender sobre la autoestima y el éxito. La esperanza de la autora es que el contenido de este libro resulte beneficioso para ti a medida que avanzas en la vida construyendo tu confianza y tu carácter.

# Virtudes: los dones interiores

| | |
|---|---|
| Asertividad | Amabilidad |
| Amor | Cariño |
| Limpieza | Lealtad |
| Compasión | Misericordia |
| Autoestima | Moderación |
| Consideración | Modestia |
| Coraje | Obediencia |
| Cortesía | Orden |
| Creatividad | Paciencia |
| Desapego | Tranquilidad |
| Determinación | Devoción |
| Entusiasmo | Decisión |
| Excelencia | Fiabilidad |
| Fidelidad | Respeto |
| Flexibilidad | Responsabilidad |
| Perdón | Reverencia |
| Amabilidad | Autodisciplina |
| Generosidad | Servicio |
| Gentileza | Firmeza |
| Diligencia | Tacto |
| Honestidad | Agradecimiento |
| Honor | Tolerancia |
| Humildad | Confianza |
| Idealismo | Cumplimiento |
| Alegría | Veracidad |
| Justicia | Unidad |

La autoestima es **para siempre**.

Va **al grano**. Aplícala a **tu vida**.

Hazlo **a tu medida**.

El credo estudiantil refleja las máximas de los cinco principios: cortesía, integridad, perseverancia, autocontrol y espíritu indomable.

## CREDO DEL ESTUDIANTE

Debo desarrollarme de manera positiva y evitar todo lo que pueda reducir mi crecimiento mental o mi salud física.

Debo desarrollar la autodisciplina para sacar lo mejor de mí mismo y de los demás.

Debo utilizar lo aprendido en clase de manera constructiva y defensiva para ayudarme a mí mismo y nunca ser abusivo con otro.

¡Los ganadores nunca se rinden!
¡Quienes se rinden nunca ganan!
¡Yo elijo ser un ganador!

Agradezco sinceramente que leas este libro. Espero que priorizar el "1,2,3, modales, etiqueta y autoestima" tenga el mismo efecto en tu vida que tuvo en la mía. Para aumentar esta probabilidad y agradecerte que hayas leído el libro, he adjuntado recursos adicionales, incluidas hojas de trabajo. Los recursos están diseñados para ayudarte a poner en práctica las ideas de este libro y para iniciar conversaciones interesantes con otras personas de tu comunidad, escuela o vecindario. Ayúdales a aprender y recordar el "1,2,3" y, por favor, mantente en contacto conmigo. Me encanta escuchar a los lectores. Siempre puedes enviarme un correo electrónico a Manners.Etiquett@yahoo.com

SEÑORA MODALES Y SEÑOR ETIQUETA

Meet The Author

# Barbara Gibson La'Grant

Barbara Gibson La'Grant, aka Ms. G, was born on November 28, 1939, in Raleigh, North Carolina, the oldest of three children and the daughter of Fred and Kathleen Jefferies.

Barbara began developing the "1 2 3" Manners, Etiquette, and Self-Esteem at various sites to include the NYCHA Community Center, Gunhill, Soundview, Parkside, Eastchester, Baychester, Pre-k teaching at the Yellow School House Baychester, her childhood school in Harlem St Marks The Evangelist School on 138th Street in Harlem, and her, location at the Ford Dealer on the corner of East 212st. Boston Rd. Bx.

Her first book, from the many columns she wrote for AL Tutt, "The Uptown Express" Its Manners Time." She also wrote for "The Bronx Times" and "The Bronx Voice" Newspaper.

She was a creative writer for her business, "ALFRBA." Among the topics she covered are "Come On Crew You Have A Job To Do, "You Know Your ABC", "Do you know your "M&E'," "123 No Obesity for "M&E", "Bullying is a "NO" joke," created with Bevin Turnbull Music Arrange and along with Veronica A De Jesus of "The New Yankee Stadium Community Benefits Funds.

Many have recognized Barbara for her talent on "The Bob Lee Show" during the Thanksgiving Holidays she presented "Manners & Etiquette." Another presentation was done on "The Patreesha's

Pot-pourri" show on Bronxnet. The King Talk Show, Real Views, Real News, and Real Talk, and The Avril Francis Show. For several years she received awards for her work as "ALFRBA" during the Tree Lighting Ceremony, given by the Honorable Larry Seabrook, Appreciation Award, also Laconia Block Association, by Alonzo de Castro.

Unity Afterschool Award for presenting "The Manners & Etiquette Workshops, for Jessie W Collins. She was the recipient of the Williamsbridge "NAACP Day Care" given the Rogers Achievement Award and recipient from Congressman Eliot Engel.

Barbara received an Achievement award from Bishop Peggy Smalls. She was honored with the Phenomenal Women's Award for 2021 Award from Coop Development by Janice Walcott, for Community Service. The Alan Carlton of Bronxnet independent filmmaker, The Film of The Manners & Etiquette with Matthew Carlton, Shakeeima Cooks, Bronx Documentary Center Film, of A day with Ms. Barbara Gibson La'Grant.

Donations from Rudy and Son Michael of Fine Fare Soundview and Ms. Lora of The Slam Dunk Hall Tremont Bx are gratefully accepted.

She is honored to have served 20 years on the Bronx Community Board 12 and received a commendation from Madam President of the Bronx Vanessa L Gibson, Congressman Jamaal Bowman. Speaker Carl E Heastie honored her service.

You will see pictures that reflect part of Ms. Barbara's journey with the Manners Etiquette Self-Esteem work she has been doing for many years here and in Appendix A. The van below was used to travel to "QBBXBKSIMAN" Queens, Bronze, Brooklyn, Staten Island, and Manhattan, often called the 5 Boroughs.

"M&E" Van Travels To You!

Ms. Barbara is recognized for her leadership and teaching Manners and Etiquette to New York City Housing Authority Children's Program.

NEW YORK CITY HOUSING AUTHORITY
90 CHURCH STREET • NEW YORK, NY 10007

TEL: 212-306-3000 • http://nyc.gov/nycha

TINO HERNANDEZ
CHAIRMAN
EARL ANDREWS, JR.
VICE CHAIRMAN
JOANNA ANIELLO
MEMBER
DOUGLAS APPLE
GENERAL MANAGER

May 18, 2005

Barbara J. Gibson
Baychester Community Center
1220 East 229th Street
Bronx, NY 10466

Dear Barbara J. Gibson,

On behalf of the New York City Housing Authority and the Department of Community Operations, I would like to take this opportunity to thank you for over 17 years of service and loyalty.

The success of NYCHA is primarily dependent on having capable employees, such as yourself, and I would like to recognize the contribution you've made in helping NYCHA provide quality service to its residents. Your passion in providing "Ms. Manners and Etiquette Training" has made a positive impression in the lives of those you have served.

Although we will miss having you as part of the team, we are extremely grateful for your years of service and offer congratulations on your retirement.

Sincerely,

Michelle R. Pinnock
Assistant Deputy General Manager
Community Operations

# Special recognition from the White House.

### Jill Biden

   The COVID-19 pandemic revealed the heart and grit of America's students, parents, and educators.  Across the Nation, the President and I have been inspired by how communities have come together to get students the support they deserve.  We are also reminded that we must build back our education system better than before.  As President Biden says, your zip code should not determine the quality of your education.  All students deserve the opportunity to learn and the support to succeed.

   As a teacher myself, I know firsthand how education can change lives. The President and I are committed to making sure that all students, all schools, and all educators have what they need, regardless of where they live.  When we invest in our students, we are investing in our Nation's future.

                    Sincerely,

                    *Jill Biden*

The White House
Washington, DC 20502

US POSTAGE
ZIP 20500
02 1W        $ 000.57⁰
0001380733 OCT

            Ms. Barbara Gibson ~ LaGrant

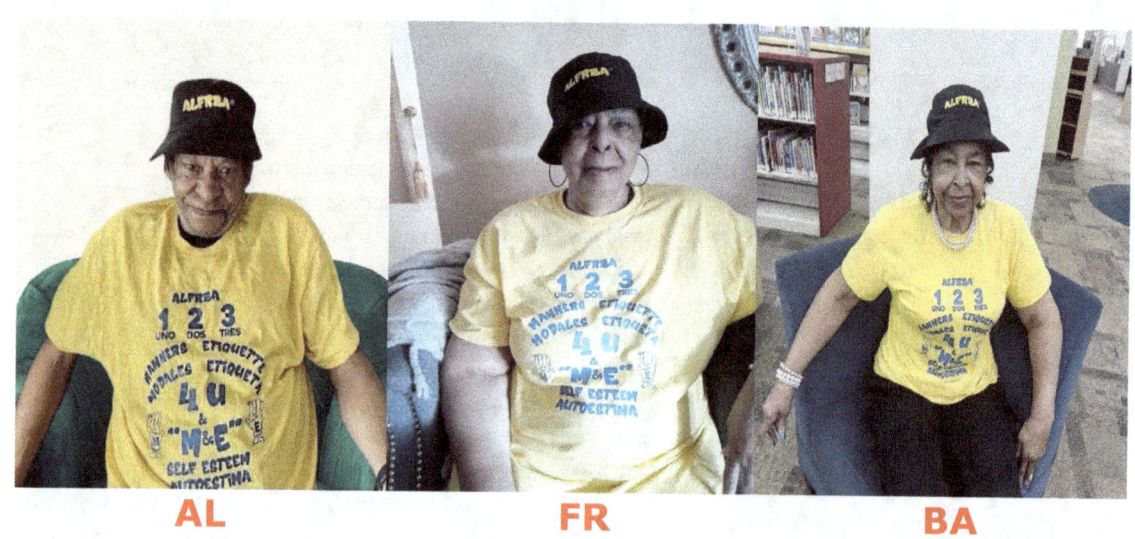

**AL**       **FR**       **BA**

Author of the book Ms. Barbara, her brother Alfred, and her sister Fredrine. The first two initials of their names create the ALFRBA (AL-FR-BA) brand.

ALFRBA Manners, Etiquette & Self-Esteem Crew

**ALFRBA Manners, Etiquette & Self-Esteem Crew**

**ALFRBA Plush "M&E"**

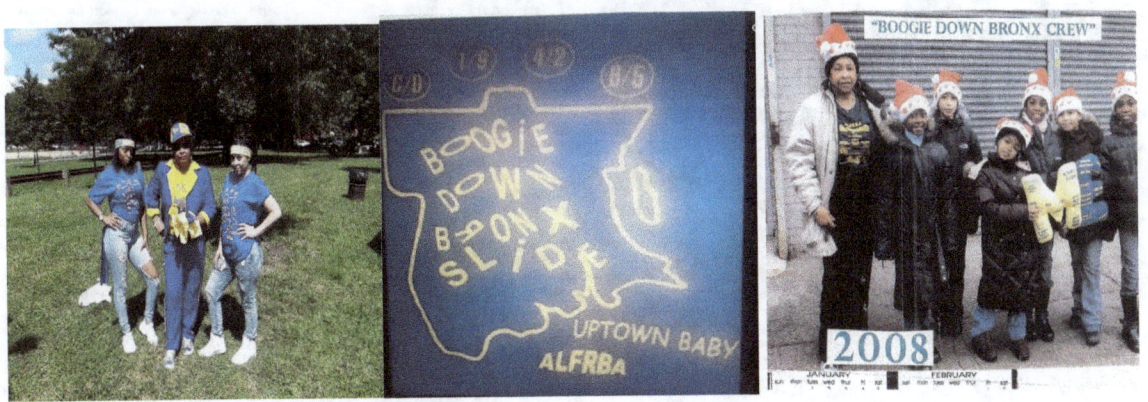

Ms. Barbara and the ALFRBA dancers performed at the "Sound View Old Timers Day" doing the Boogie Down Bronze Slide. Also, her Boogie Down Crew.

# Mind your Ps & Qs

## Bronx woman on mission to teach children good manners

BY TIZIANA RINALDI

"What time is it?" Barbara Gibson-La Grant pointedly asked her students. "It's manners time!" answered the cheerful group that has been faithfully attending Gibson-La Grant's workshops on social graces.

Ms. G, as she is affectionately called in her Northwest Bronx community, is known for her conviction that good manners are forever — a very serious topic that should be taught to children on a regular basis. Her passion has long fueled a tireless

advocacy for the cause of polite and respectful kids.

"Our children are not using manners and etiquette as often as they should," said Gibson-La Grant, a retired community coordinator for NYCHA whose free manners and etiquette courses are designed to enrich the lives of less privileged kids, particularly ages six to 16.

Gibson-La Grant said the practice of manners and etiquette was instilled in her by a mother who wanted "well-raised New Yorkers." Later in life she

honed that knowledge by refining her education and pursuing independent research to develop tools and curricula that she has taken to community centers and after-school programs in the Bronx, Harlem and other parts of New York City.

"I tell my students that kings and queens train their children, Puff Daddy and Donald Trump train [their] kids, and I train [them] because [they] are little kings and queens," said Gibson-La Grant, who believes that this type of grooming is critical to social upward mobility. The Williamsbridge branch of the NAACP recently honored her for her decades of community involvement and her extensive work in support of Bronx children.

Explaining that manners — saying "please" and "thank you" — are considered social skills, while rules of etiquette — knowing how to use your napkin at the table — are life skills, Gibson-La Grant feels that what modern children need the most is to understand basic instructions. That is, of course, beside avoiding all-time no-no's such as cursing, chewing with their mouths open or not offering their seat to an elderly person on the train.

"I teach my students that we must respect words," she said. "When someone tells you to stop, you must stop, because it can save your life."

Children must be taught to listen, she emphasized, so they can promptly correct their behavior. The community teacher has developed several props, including two pillows in the shape of an M, for "manners," and an E, for "etiquette," a board game and a rap song called "Come on crew we have a job to do," to get her point across.

On the other end of the spectrum, another powerful word often forgotten by today's youth is "yes."

"Many say 'yeah'," pointed out Gibson-La Grant, who has plenty of field experience not only as a teacher, but also as the mother of five and the grandmother of seven.

"I [emphasize] not to use their head or their shoulders, but to use the word 'yes.'" Should the habit per-

sist, it may make a difference on a jo[b] interview down the line, she warned.

Students practice manners or et[i]quette rules during sessions wher[e] they are either educated about a cho[o]sen topic, or polish their behavio[r] using mishaps that come up durin[g] class interaction. After all, "[people] make mistakes as [they] are together," said Gibson-La Grant, and her stu[dents seem to take well to that.

"I think that children need mor[e] manners," 9-year-old Jada Brown sai[d] candidly. The girl, who attends P[S] 41, is a regular at Gibson-La Grant'[s] classes. "Some walk down the bloc[k] saying words that aren't in the vo[cabulary, like 'ain't,' or 'yeah.' The[y] [sound] like they have no home train[ing!"

"A lot of my friends curse, scream at each other, and it is not appropri[ate for anybody," said Amber Dropp, [a] middle school student who travels t[o] Gibson-La Grant's classes from Co-o[p] City. She likes to learn about manners and etiquette because, she says, [it] will help her "go places in life."

Media, such as rap music, doesn'[t] help matters.

"People like to hear nasty saying[s] and words," said Gibson-La Grant. She wants to tap into children's love of media by releasing an educationa[l] video on manners and etiquette in collaboration with her student[s] and MS 142, the Philip Sousa middl[e] school, where she frequently offer[s] her programs.

Aside from her classes, keeping u[p] the lessons learned is key. Gibson-L[a] Grant, who also trains adults for free, said parents must reinforce their chil[dren's good manners at home.

"Those who know the rules o[f] [proper conduct] should reinforc[e] them with their children, and fo[r] those who don't, find out the answers so when your children go out they wil[l] represent you well," she said.

*Barbara Gibson-La Grant workshops* (718) 881-3809.

*"Manners on Etiquette" community* *workshop [Gun Hill Playground, Ma[genta Street and Holland Avenue, at th[e] end of July. Call for exact date, not avail[able at press time (646) 765-8816].*

# Community activist teaches youth social skills

**Bronx Times**
BY STEVEN GOODSTEIN
October 2-8, 2015

A long-time Bronx community activist is teaching our youth the principles of good manners and proper etiquette.

Barbara Gibson La Grant has dedicated her life to helping children improve their social skills.

She earned a Masters in Child Care at Child Care, Inc. now known as the Center for Children's Initiatives.

It was around this time that Gibson La Grant first observed that many children she interacted with lacked social ability.

During her 20-year career working for the NYC Housing Authority she further observed the poor social interactions between today's youth.

For example, she would notice that many kids would not say "please" and "thank you", and would say "yeah" instead of the appropriate "yes", when responding to someone.

This led Barbara to transform Alfrba, originally a 1960's designer company she created in her post-graduate years, into an organization geared towards teaching youth about social manners and life skills in 2011.

The workshops conducted through Alfrba for kids, ages 7 to 15, introduce them to proper table manners, such as how to set the table with utensils, as well as how to clap during live events.

Manners, etiquette and self-esteem workshops take place every Thursday and Friday from 3 to 6 p.m. at 3325 Boston Road on the corner of 211th Street.

Students that graduate the course attend an event at Eastwood Manor to receive an Alfrba certificate.

Gibson La Grant has incorporated her designer skills into furthering her goals.

She created a set of two pillows shaped in an 'M' (for manners) and an 'E' (for etiquette) that include polite words and phrases in both English and Spanish.

She is currently working with a manufacturer to market the bilingual pillows to deliver her message to more youth.

"In today's society, everybody, especially the younger generation, is used to communicating either through cell phones or other electronic devices, so 'every other form of communication has become obsolete," Gibson La Grant said.

"That is why it is important not to forget how to properly communicate, person to person, and continue to develop and keep these social life skills, young or old."

The North Carolina native has trademarked and copyrighted her business with the help of Start Small Think Big.

Gibson La Grant poses with her bilingual pillows, the 'M' pillow stands for 'manners' and the 'E' pillow stands for 'etiquette'.
*Photo courtesy of Alfrba*

"They (SSTB) taught me how to make my business go in the right direction. I would never have gotten this far without them," she added.

"Barbara has devoted a lot of time and energy to the youth of the community, and she has made a big impact on their lives," said Fredtrine Jefferies, Barbara's sister, who also acts as Alfrba's vice president. "She loves those kids, loves guiding them, and the reward she receives for her hard work is seeing these kids mature and grow up - which makes it all worth it to her."

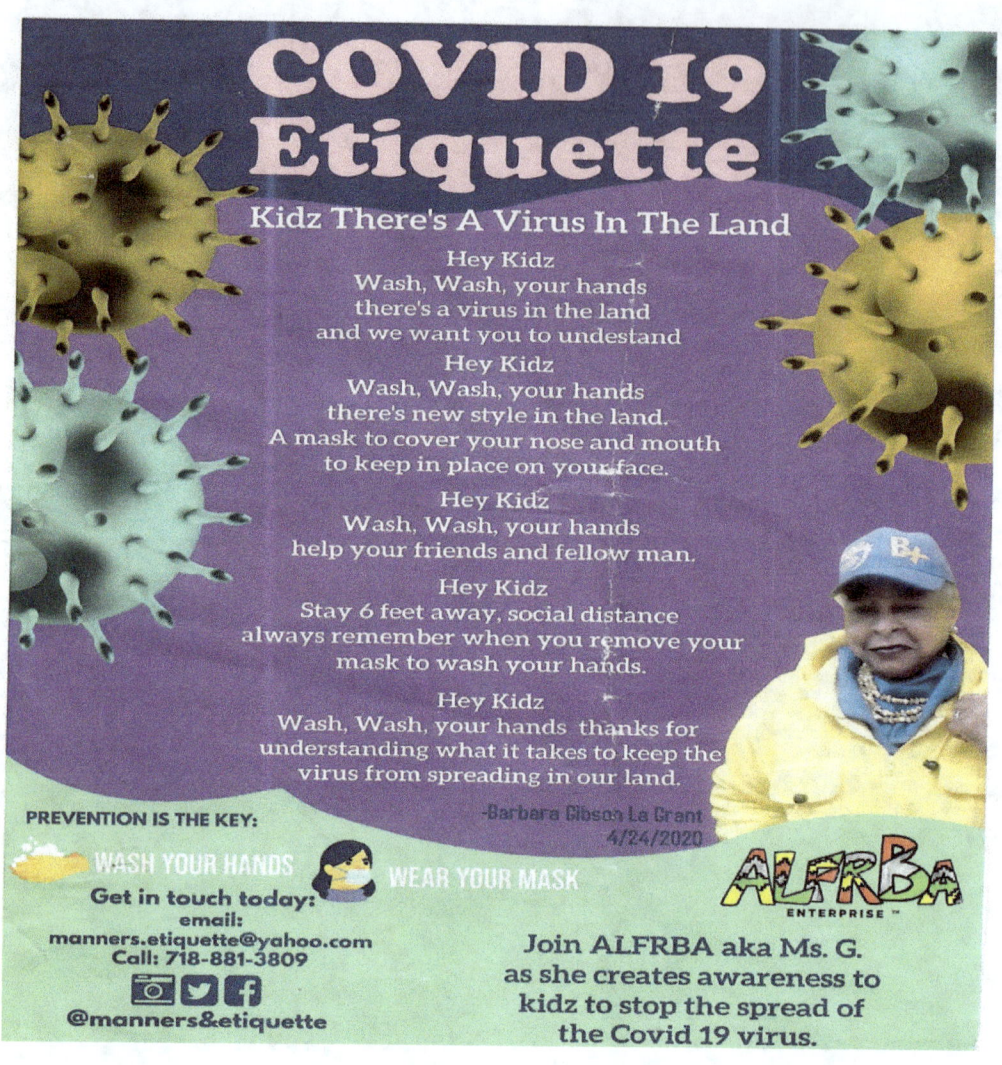

172

The Many Faces of Ms. Barbara

Appendices

# Appendix A

## Friends and family that support this book

**Minister, Entertainers, and BX Politicians**

**Superstars & Politicians**

More Family & Friends Support For This Book.

# Barbara's Family & Friends

Special recognition to her brother, shown in uniform above, Alfred of ALFRBA for being "Best of the Best Top Solider Bronze Star C.I.B. Expert Combat Vietnam 69-70" Fort Jackson, South Carolina.

My Author Friend's

Betty J. Murray                Felecia La'Grant

Attending Worship & Event with Friends

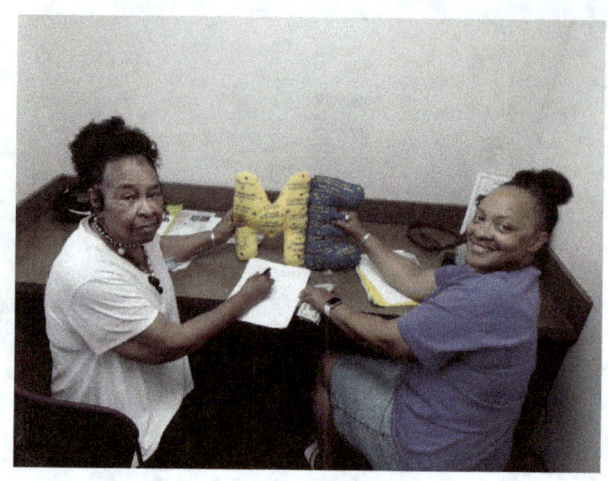

JATNE Publishing
Thank you to Mrs. Hicks for connecting me to my agent, Dr. Annette West.

Finally, with all my love, to my husband and in memory of my son and nephew.

# Appendix B

## Special Recognitions "Thank You"

With so many supporting Barbara, aka Ms. G "ALFRBA," she wishes to share a special thank you to the following honorable people.

Thanks to Peter A. Contreras, Harold Bendell, at the Ford Dealer on the corner of East 212st. Boston Rd. Bx.

Thanks to Walter Pofeldt, David Greene, for the many pictures they did, making sure "ALFRBA CREW" were in the spotlight.

To the Members of Board 12, George L. Torres, Ursula Greene, Robert Hall, Jonnie Goff, Alfredo Figueroa, Thank God Adeyemi La Crown II, Myishia Taylor-Myke, Clinton A. Myke, Carla Borsotti, Karl Stricker, Dena Robin, Ann Larrier, Shaneque E. Moore, H. Hilary Bloomfield, Pamela Hamilton-Johnson, Bro Brown. Ted James, Anthony Ried, John Isaac. I appreciate you all and our time working together.

Thank you, Ivan Anthony Borras, much love for your support.

Thank you, Ruben Diaz, Sr, Former Bronx Borough President Ruben Diaz, Jr. Jose M. Serrano, Eliot Engel, Jamaal Bailey, Kevin C. Riley, Jamaal Bowman, Andy King, Marcos A. Crespo, Darcel D. Clark, Madame Vanessa L. Gibson Bronx Borough President. Hugh W. Campbell, Jason Laidley, Alexandrae Wint, Brian Melford, Alina K. Dowe, Kenny Agosto, Cynthia Cox, Dominique Maddox, Joel Rivera, and Elvin Garcia, for your support.

To Speaker Carl E. Heastie for his support of the "Kids, There Is A Virus In The Land." Also, thankful to the Granby Family for their support in believing "M&E."

To Master Artist Richard Sisco "Sisco Kid" who made "ALFRBA" design & more, to his friend Victor Valente and his Brother, the Artist also Darral Sisco who carries on the work for "ALFRBA" to make "M&E" what it is today.

To supporters since the beginning of "M&E" thanks to By LOLY, Balbina J. Guity, Pamela Jackson, Dennis Kupperman, and to Betty Murray, thank you in giving "M&E" the idea to make "Napkins" to be part of Conversational Plush" items.

Special thanks to the Community Supporter Chery Dewitt, Kathleen Y. Branch, Sherene Hall, Sophia Reid, Jim Alston, Brenda Moreira, Lady Pamela, Priscilla Crowell, Michelle Chapman, Hattie Jones, Carolyn Kentockee, Debra Longhorn, Mary Cabrera, Wheatley Davis, Antonia D. Exum, Veronica Exum, Roselle Hayward, Angie Williams, Dorothy Febus, Suzie Yvette Olmo-Gonzaies, Karen Nichson, Damon Anthony, Eddie Stevens, Anthony G. Horne. Dorothy Spence, "Our Tina the Ballerina" without a doubt, is our Tina Monique James, Doctor of Public Health, that our family are proud of.

To the love of Basketball, thank you to my Brother Alfred Jefferies who played in different Basketball Tournaments Bronxdale, Bronxriver, and Soundview. I learned to support other teams in my community because of him and with the support of Larry Seabrook and Adrian Armstrong, I started the Gun Hill Basketball Teams. With the help of Nathan (Nat) Ramos, we made the first game's T-shirt G.T.A. Also, thanks to Nestor, Glenn, Shahid, Esther Grant, Darryl Lockhart in continuing working with, The Gun Hill Basketballs Classic for many years, to Clarence (Mugsy) Meggett, to one of those pioneers in basketball as a mentor to inner NYC youth. Shout to Bro Teach, from basketball to football, Carlos of T.I.M.O., for working with the kids and making a difference in our community in keeping Gun Hill on the map. Dexter Gardiner, and Twin Derrick RIP pleased me to meet Mike Tyson, the heavy-weight boxer.

From the Block, Thank you to Shirley Tripicco, Shirley Bennette, Michael Simm, Clayton Jones, Ronald Lee, Kevin Cherry, Dwight Cherry, Demetria Cherry, Yolanda Gray, Renee Howell, Elaine Johnson, Michelle Gibbs, Hyllaree Moore, Kevin Meggett, Sammie Hawkins, Larry Thomas, Jimmy Hair Stylist, God Son Carl Wright, God Daughter, Carolyn Dion Landon.

To Jonathan La' Grant 3, Constantia La'Grant Gundy-Gallishaw, Jonathan La'Grant Gundy Jr, Jabah La'Grant Gundy, Love Ms. G.

To the "ALFRBA" Dance, Ana Rokafella Garcia, the full circle "Souliaha Dance Company" for helping create "The Boogie Down Bronx Slide" Part two, Thanks Marilyn Patterson for the choreographing step of "The Boogie Down Bronx Slides" that I wrote and perform with the "ALFRBA" dancer Deana Richline, and Jennifer "Beasty Acosta."  The music by "Cover" ALL Ave MAA. Remix Delvin Brown.

To my Super Star, "Will TRAXX" Voice of the City, Also known for. "Let Me See Some Foot Work", Lord Tariq De ja Vu, the hip Rapp.

er (Uptown Baby) D.J. Tariq Nelson, Damion Anthony, Kit Kat Nat, Lonnie Youngblood, and so grateful to Michael Graham for getting to the Apollo 125th Street in Harlem to see "Fat Joe" and receiving his book The "Book of Jose."

Yes, still more to thank. The "ALFRBA" Kidz and Parent Sherri Yancey, Lady Jenine, Joel Martey, Naa- Morkor Martey, Destiny Baltimore, Tricia Campbell, Alaysia Williams, Anita Katou Kouami, Emmanuela Katou Kouami, Curtis Katou Koua, Akwugo O. Dimoriaku, Daachiobi N. Dimoriaku, Mmachi O Dimoriaku, Benedicta N. Kechi Dimoriaku, Nia Joseph, Natasha Davis, Debbie Davis, Vanessa Jones, Maritza

Hernandez, Summer, Winter Exum, Sophie, Skylar Jefferies, Jayden, Haylei, and Hydea Jefferies, Ji' Hanem Hawkins, Ariah Borras, Shane Farrington, Nyasia, Talaysia and Ty'varius Wright, and Da'vya Spann.

Special Thanks to Nikim Brown, Tanieke Farrington, Genaea Miller, Linda Mack, Sherry Jackson, Chanda Wright, Rosa D. Jones, Mari Groomes, Anita Gamble, Ululy Rafael Martinez, Sherman Browne, Shirley Saunders, Felicia La'Grant.

Barbara Facebook Family: Michael Max Knobbe, Jim Alston, Joan Melford, Samuel Granby, Ayris B. Granby, Fat Joe, AL Sharpton, Grandmaster Caz, Mele Mel Glover, Mike Lawrence, James Catto, Scottie Cabrera, Dimitri Hinton, Angelo Hinton, Linda Bailey, Julie M. Jeffers, Theresa Horne, Andre Collins, Teena Small, Regina Archer, Andy Lee, Willie Hudson, Michael Felter, LaToya Niles, Keith Ramsey, Keisha Keish Burgess, T Burgess, Shane Gaymon, Cedric Gaymon, Corey Montgomery, Cliff Montgomery, Marlene Sutherland, Turhan Sutherland, Diana Pearson, Joseph Pearson, Derek K. Cason, Anatonia Cason, Bettie Cole, Jerome A. Thompson Jr, Fernando Cabrera, Patricia Grant, Robert Cumberbatch, Juan Tavarez  Vives, Izzy Rivera, Ricky Rivera, Russell Holloway, Lorenzo Ganaway, Lyndon Wright, Sunshine Quotes from the Heart. Howard Holland, Lisa Knox, Murices Wilson, Gail Green, Valerie White, Jennie Hall, Carolle York, Ed  Smith, Marva York,  Barbara Leak-Walkins, Jacquelyn Cauthen, Charles Powell, Fern Powell-Hockaday, Chanda Le' Grant, Betty La' Grant, Larry La' Grant , Thomas La' Grant, Rebecca La' Grant, Jerome La' Grant, Hilda Gerena-Diaz, Nene Ali, Neva Shillingford-King, Kia Gai, Kenneth Stelley, Alfred Jefferies Jr, Erica Jenkins-Jefferies, Jayden Jefferies, Diane Jefferies, Ellie Minor, Jay W. Mc Kenzie, Rocky Bucano, Kyleer Bucano, Papsi Rosario, Anthony Cromer, Joyce Cromer, Debra Marrow, Cheri Taylor, E'lyse Murray, Walter Miller, Ann Larrier, Jeanette Walker, Marlene Smith, Patrica Grant, Terri Ham, Sugar Best, Sheila Jones, Velvet Vinnie, Shannon, Romeo, Robby, and Gregory Lockhard.

Bishop Peggie Small, Reverend Lamont S. Granby, Pastor Jay Gooding Sr. Rabbi Keith Thompson, Minister Kwame Thompson.

Thank you to THE PARENT GROUP FOR GUNHILL: Irma Gray, Virginia Evan, Charlotte Trafton, Loretta And Cleave Harris, Lula Hawkins, Wenceslaea Martinez, Helen Hearn Kelly, Vance, Tyson, and D.J. Doug Gibbs

Thanks to Bronx Ball Friend, Adaline Walker Santiago for getting our tickets.

Thanks to my phone friend Luciel Boles-Wilson for always being available for me.

Magie Ortiz kept me looking good like Ms. G. Bx was supposed to be. To My Jeweler, Patricia Castillo, and my dressmaker, I appreciate you both. Also, to Cassandra Gundy for doing my makeup.

To my cousin Carston Exum that (Sale Book) now I have one for him to sell, thank you for all your information.

Thanks to THE PARENT OF PARKSIDE, Patricia (Pat) Wright, Saria Wright, and Mildred (Millie) Harding, for her Poem "Why the Parkside Kids Love, MS G."

At BAYCHESTER: Jean Mickelson, My Maid of Honor as my right-hand person on my Wedding Day, Nov 5. 2005 with Love, Thank You.

Thanks to Bronx Dale Project, known as (Sotomayor Houses) where I started then Sound View, was the beginning of opening my eye to see the need for "Manners & Etiquette Self Esteem" ALFRBA "M&E'!

BRONXDALE PROJECT: To the many families that I was their babysitter to earn money. Also to the family friends, The Cromer, Archers, Best, McKinnon, Jamison,

185

Carrol, Brown, Roberson, Cooper, Turpin, Ames, Simmons, Barr, (P.A.L) Bailey, Washington, Brown, Freeman, Singleton, Lawrence, Hine, Edwards, Ellington and to my school friends, Audrey White, Betty O' Neil, Annette Freeman, Marilyn Brown.  And to Barbara Trent and I enjoyed meeting the Famous (doo-hop) Group "The Harp tones", William (Demp) Dempsey, and our own "HIP HOP" Star OF 1715 Bruckner Blvd, "Disco King Mario" I will always remember you playing your music under my mother's window; making history, as you are well-known today.

To many others that I am thankful for today.

Unity Women Support Group, Jessie W. Collins, Karen Nichson.

Mind Your Own Business, NYCHA

Honorable Ruben Diaz's Sound View in Action, "Coca-Cola", First Xmas Parade in the Bronx with "FAT JOE" & "ALFRBA CREW," Ruben Diaz Jr. and Afrika Bambaataa.

Bronx Hunts Point Entrepreneur Women's Program, Josephine Infante.

Shout out to Anthony Diamond Caribbean, musical star.

Start Small Think Big Small Business Resources, Jenny Da Silva.

Monroe Entrepreneur Program, George L. Acevedo, and Marcia Cameron, thank you for that extra time to copyright "ALFRBA Boogie Down Bronx Uptown Baby" LLC.  The business starts on APRIL 1, 2000, to my lawyer Auten Matthew R, I welcome your (free service). Thank you, Thank you.

Thank you to 47 Precinct Explores Director, Amelia Patric.  You had the Manners & Etiquette workshop for the young men and women being introduced to a career in law or the criminal justice system. I am honored to have had a part in teaching social skills to many; that was a blessing for "M&E."

A Great Grand Special thanks to the support staff at the Sumter Library; Charles, Susan, Greg, and Aaron. First floor, Keanna, Randi, Brenda, Nancy, Julie, Andrea, Nipa, Jonathan, and Drew, who cleaned each day. You all assisted me in this last year and wished me good outcomes for this book.

I thank Clarence and George E., who I met at the library for their encouragement.

Thanks, Towanda Hick, Chantea Williams, for guiding me to JATNE Publishing, where I have worked with Dr. Annette West on this book. It's been a long journey, but we are excited to be at the end of this road.

Also, thanks to creative artist Marie Lyriq for her support.

Finally, thanks to Ariel Gamble, my great cousin, for representing "Manners Etiquette Self-Esteem 4 "U" & "M&E" Book and *Keeping My Legacy Alive*.

# Appendix C

## I CAN GET WITH IT!

RAP LYRICS. By Fredtrine A. Jeffries "ALFRBA"

Manners are forever, they go a long way.
It's not about who you are, what you wear,
But what you do and say. Can you get with it?
I can get with it.

Manners are forever, leads you on an upward path,
Separates you from the riff raff.
Can you get with it? I can get with it.

Manners are forever, use them in every way, be polite to
an old lay, make her day.
Can you get with it? I can get with it.

Manners are forever, do things that you can be proud of an
cherish don't let manners perish.
Can you get with it? I can get with it.

Manners are forever, at home, in school, even at play, get turned on to doing
things with good manners today.
Can you get it? I can get it.

# Appendix D

## MANNERS SONG

### 2001, Barbara Gibson La'Grant

Come on crew, we have a job to do (Job to do)/ Remember…You too.
We have a place in society too—
You know they're watching what we do and say.
We need to get our acts - together – with no delay.

When you drop trash on the ground
You can't be down –'Cause you're making more of a mess.
Becoming less than your best in society.
You need to stop when there's a garbage can over there – see.

You need to change things around, like your attitude.
There's no need to be mean or just be rude.
You're the future of the world, and you need to show.
That your intelligence is strong and has room to grow.

Chorus Two

Proper phrases like please and thank you in return—
are necessary when someone has given what you earned.
May I, excuse me, especially when you pass –
leave you feeling dignity, pride, and even class.

Why don't you do these things and you'll find it's true.
It's your world, and you have a lot of things to do.

Chorus
Keep it real ya'll—
Actions speak louder than words.
Respect yourself so that it's seen and it's heard.
Keep it real—give respect where respect is due.
Be proud of society and make it proud of you.

**MANNERS & ETIQUETTE**

**SEÑORA MODALES Y SEÑOR ETIQUETA**

www.ingramcontent.com/pod-product-compliance
Lightning Source LLC
Chambersburg PA
CBHW081327120626
46546CB00011B/3251